Paranormal Mysteries of Eurasia
Volume I

Paranormal Mysteries of Eurasia

Volume I

Paul Stonehill

2011
Galde Press, Inc.
Lakeville, Minnesota, U.S.A.

Paranormal Mysteries of Eurasia: Vol. I

Printed in the United States of America

First Edition

Second Printing, 2014

cover design by Chris Mattox and Chee Vang

Galde Press, Inc.
PO Box 460
Lakeville, Minnesota 55044–0460

www.galdepress.com

Contents

Part One
Lost Treasures of Eurasia

Chapter 1

Born of Celestial Fire
The Story of Ginseng

THE HEALING QUALITIES of ginseng (*jen shen*) have been surrounded by legends for many centuries. It has been called the Wonder Root, the Gift of the Gods, the Root of Life, and the Elixir of Immortality. It has been used by traditional Chinese medicine for more than two thousand years (there are ancient Chinese medical manuscripts about it dating back to 2800 B.C.). Ginseng possesses incredible life potential. Today, the true Chinese ginseng (*Panax ginseng*) that grows in the Russian Far East (the Primorye) is a rare and unique plant. It grows in the Ussurian taiga, a singularly beautiful place, where nature is abundant and biodiversity is tremendous in its scope (no wonder it is called the "northern jungle").

Ginseng is fragile and small, but also strong, and after being injured, the plant can lie in the soil for many years, and then grow again in a new body. A twenty-year-old plant only has three leaves; if it reaches the venerable age of sixty years, it has five leaves. *Jen shen* blossoms in July, and tiny red berries appear in August. The Wonder Root does not like sunlight. It grows in areas where the rays of the sun never penetrate. *Jen shen* can be found in hanging valleys with steep terrain and abundant snowfall. It loves cedar trees, and lets its root grow under them. Many people seek true ginseng, but only Chinese sages know its full medicinal value.

Medical Research of *Panax ginseng*

The genus name *Panax* means "cure-all" in Greek. In 1843 Carl Meyer, a Russian botanist, gave the *Panax ginseng* term to ginseng.

The chemical composition of ginseng is well known, but scientists have not been very successful in their efforts to replicate it. Although ginseng has been researched extensively, its curative mechanism is not understood in the West; nevertheless, Western medicine has accepted it as a medicinal herb.

Ginseng is characterized as a mild stimulant and an adapter (a preparation helping the organism to adapt to an unfavorable environment). It is said to be very effective in the treatment of nervous and mental diseases; it is also believed to influence carbohydrate metabolism by lowering the content of sugar in the blood, improve functions of the sexual glands, help eyesight, fight viruses, boost immunity, reduce cholesterol, improve mental and physical capacity for work, and treat colds. It is said to have rejuvenating powers.

One of the lesser-known properties of *jen shen* is its ability to fight excess body weight. Ancient Chinese manuscripts mentioned ginseng's catabolic properties.

Interesting studies have been conducted in the Laboratory of Biotechnology of the Institute of Biology and Soil Science (Far East Branch) of the Russian Academy of Sciences. A gene of rhizogene bacteria was built into the DNA composition of a ginseng strain cell. This led to numerous variations in the morphological, hormonal, and biosynthetic characteristics of ginseng cells. The original ginseng cells into which the gene was transferred originated from the stalk. After transformation, they could form roots, leaves, and even flowers.

Nowadays, there are many predators who roam the taiga trying to find and grab this fragile, wonderful, little-understood but long-revered treasure of planet Earth.

Secret Rituals and Ancient Knowledge

Ancient legends hold that the gods hide the Wonder Root from the masses, and show it only to those who are worthy.

Chinese medical science has used ginseng as a cure for many illnesses. When traveling in the wintertime, the Chinese carried the root with them to provide warmth and prevent hunger. They believed it cured five internal organs, subdued arrogance and anger, calmed people down, and saved them from the evil eye. People close to death could be revived by drinking a potion made from the Root of Life. A Chinese pharmacology textbook from A.D. 1596, Li Shi-Zhen's *Grand Materia Medica* (*Ben cao gan mu*), included over one hundred prescriptions for drugs prepared from *jen shen*.

The search for *jen shen* was organized on a national level in China during the Manchurian dynasty, and trained groups of people in special uniforms, dubbed "blue pheasants," looked for the Root of Life in forests. Behind them marched Imperial soldiers and officials, lest they steal the *jen shen*.

To harm the root meant severe punishment; finding the true ginseng resulted in rich rewards.

The Udegei people, who live in villages throughout the Primorye, are true natives of the land, and traded *jen shen* (or *pan-tsui* in their language) to the Chinese, who had overtaken their lands but later ceded them to the Russians.

The Russians first learned the value of *jen shen* from the Chinese *manza* (seekers) who began to cross the border when their resources diminished. Those *manza* led a difficult existence full of dangers among deep forests and faraway mountains. Their gaze was usually cast downward as a habit; they were ascetic people with keen senses. They were as agile as tigers, had the eyesight of hawks, and could smell and hear the dangers of the taiga as well as wolves and hares. But they never lost their human essence among the struggles with wild nature. They faced death constantly and were fatalistic, but believed in destiny and trusted that mountain and taiga spirits would assist them in their quest to find the Root of Life. They also knew that more dangerous than any animal was another human being, waiting for them in ambush, a predator with a gun in his hand.

According to the renowned Russia explorer V. Arsenyev, the skilled *manza*, upon seeing the ginseng, threw away his staff and, covering his eyes, fell down on the ground. "Do not leave, *pan-tsui*," he would scream loudly. "I am a pure person, my soul has been freed from sins, my heart is open, and I have no evil intentions." Only then would the Chinese or Udegei seeker be bold enough to open his eyes and look at the plant.

The location where the plant is found is diligently searched and studied. The *manza* looks at the topography, the geological composition of the surrounding area, the soil, and the various plants. He determines the location of the sun in relation to the ginseng plant, and the flow of the wind. After observing the area, the *manza* gets down on his knees, moves the grass aside, and very carefully looks at the plant. When he determines that the

ginseng plant is solitary, and no other of the kind is at the site, the *manza* carefully excavates the ground, barely uncovering the plant. By looking at its wrinkles and the grooves, the *manza* determines its quality. If he decides that the root is still small, he lets it grow until the next year. In that case, the *manza* makes sure he returns it and the site to the order he found it in. If the *pan-tsui* is in the stage of blossoming or the maturation of its seeds, the *manza* lets it blossom and drop its seeds so other plants can grow. Thin wooden sticks surround the *pan-tsui* itself, a sign that the root has been found there. No other Chinese *manza* would ever touch it. The taiga keeps many secrets. But people who dwell there know that in the past he who stole *jen shen* from another person's territory was buried alive and left to die.

One who seeks the Root of Life cannot carry weapons. According to the ancient legends, *jen shen* loves only peaceful people whose hearts are pure. Those who find the Wonder Root cannot reject it, for misfortune would follow them.

When the time comes, the root is extracted from the soil with all necessary precautions.

Other Russian sources mention that the Chinese ginseng seekers (*wa-pan-tsui*) developed their own secret language (*hao-shu-hoa*), special tree signs, and various marks to indicate the areas where roots were excavated and the characteristics of the seeds. They would find a cedar tree close to the site and cut out a piece of the bark. Then they would wrap a moss-covered *jen shen* plant into the bark. One year later, the wood tar that came out of the cut would be burned. As a result, there appeared the so-called "black burns," clearly visible in the taiga; they served as a "news board" about roots found in the area.

Russian seekers call it *lobaderina* in their secret vernacular.

The ancient custom of covering the *jen shen* roots with moss and placing them in a special box made from the bark of a coniferous tree had a very deep meaning. The root was protected against injuries and infections. Many microorganisms that cause the *pan-tsui* root to become ill are always present in the soil. When the soil is undisturbed, such microorganisms are either inactive, or in a state of saprotroph (an organism that obtains its nutrients from non-living organic matter, usually dead and decaying plant or animal matter, by absorbing soluble organic compounds). As the soil gets disturbed due to the excavation and so on, they become active and can damage the precious root. Hence, the *manza* and *wa-pan-tsui* use moss, a well-known antiseptic. (During numerous wars, moss was used to disinfect wounds, and the water that engulfs moss never decays.)

Some *manza* also kept the Root of Life in wooden boxes during the day.

Modern Russian ginseng seekers (not the predatory poachers) are called *kornevschiki* (*koren'* means "root" in Russian). They follow the ancient Chinese traditions of the Wonder Root seekers. They walk the taiga in a strictly maintained row with a precise distance between them. They carry *soborgoon* (a special staff used to seek the *jen shen* and chase away snakes). They break the branches of young trees to mark the area and do not go back there again. Thorough searches often produce sightings of the so-called "dog *pan-tsui*," any plant that has red berries. But the genuine *jen shen* is very hard to find.

The *kornevschiki* have a secret vocabulary of their own. They use ancient Chinese terms to distinguish the Wonder Root (*pochanza* is a plant with one leaf, *al'taza* with two, *tantaza* with three, *sipiye* with four, *upiye* with five, and *lipiye* with the very rare six leaves).

The leaves resemble a human hand.

The largest roots have their own names (The Ussuriyan Old Man, and others). The larger the root the more expensive it is. Two-hundred-gram roots are rare; those of four hundred to six hundred grams are unique and almost impossible to find. The root of genuine *jen shen* resembles a human being, and the taiga *manza* gave its parts anatomical names (the main root is called the "body"). There are "female" and "male" roots.

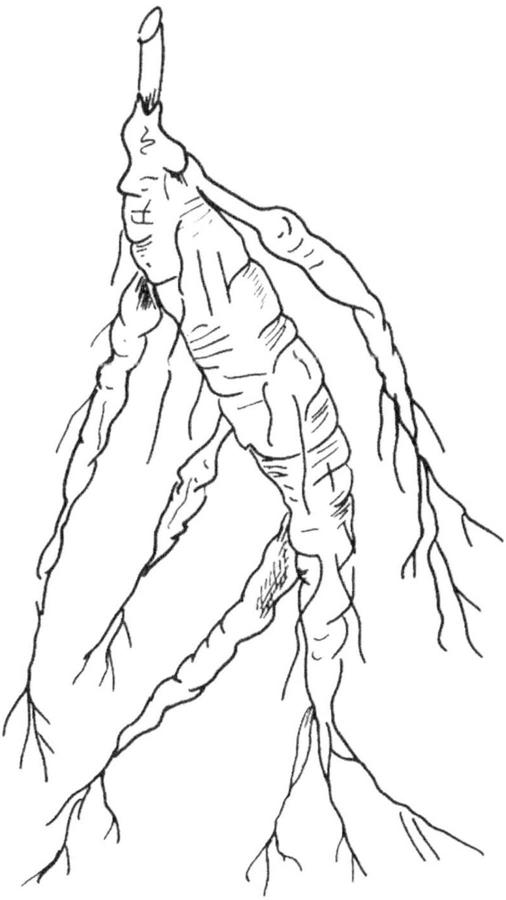

The ginseng root.

The *kornevschiki* believe in supernatural powers that guard the Wonder Root, and speak the secret language with the taiga spirits. Some, like the Udegei, worship *bua*, the master spirit of the Ussurian taiga. They read the *lobaderina* signs found in the bark of the cedar trees and strike them with their *soborgoon* a number of times as their traditions demand.

Their taiga language includes cuts in the trees, signs carved in stone, and mounds built from small rocks; in the past some signs belonged to their family clans and were truly secret. They knew how to warn others whom they trusted of the dangers in a given area.

The *kornevschiki* kill poisonous, deadly snakes that lurk in the grass and among rocks. An ancient belief has it that once the poisonous reptile is killed, one can find the *jen shen*; the explanation lies in the fact that one really strains his eyes safeguarding against the snakes and thus develops keen vision.

The Chinese claimed that the Root of Life was of supernatural origins. Long ago lightning struck a clear mountain brook. The water disappeared, and in the spot where when lightning struck, a plant appeared imbued with the strength of "celestial fire." Yet another legend tells the story of a root called *jen shen* that lived in China long ago and had the ability to turn into human beings and animals. The great Chinese prophet Lao Tse discovered its healing, curative strength and gave the people its description. The *jen shen* was disturbed by this and hid in the North, where another Chinese scientist, using herbs, found its whereabouts.

There is yet another legend about the origins of the Root of Life, and it also comes from China. Chinese villagers once heard strange sounds coming from the ground; they resembled a prayer or a call for help from under the surface. At the place where the sounds were the loudest, the peasants discovered a small plant. It was carefully excavated, and they found a strange-looking root, whose shape resembled that of a human being. That is why they called it *jen shen*. They believed it embodied the spirit of the Earth.

Jen Shen in the 21st Century

Panax ginseng, the Root of Life, is on the verge of extinction.

Many Russian dwellers of the taiga grow ginseng at home and later replant it in taiga soil. They hope that the plant will combine traits of the taiga-grown ginseng, and there will be a morphological similarity. They plant seeds, as well as five-year-old *jen shen*; it goes through an illness stage, and continues its growth. Poverty has driven many Russians into the taiga to seek out *jen shen* and sell it to Chinese buyers. The transplantation can produce a significant, baneful effect on the gene pool of the wild-growing population of *Panax ginseng*.

Chinese and Russian criminal groups have been organized that smuggle Siberian tigers, wildlife derivatives, gold, drugs, women, and the Root of Life from the Primorye to China.

Russia used to be the main supplier of the wild and planted ginseng, but lost the lead to South Korea and the United States. Centuries of *jen shen* gathering have truly exhausted its reserves; and to assure supply, Koreans began its cultivation over five hundred years ago.

"Siberian ginseng," popular in the West, is not a genuine *jen shen*. It grows in the Ussurian taiga, where it is called *eleuthererococcus*. This plant is a distant botanical relative of true ginseng. It is less popular than *pan-tsui* and is a distinct plant with different active chemical components, used in preparation of both medicines and foodstuffs.

In the 1980s, the Soviets researched plant growth in space aboard their space stations. Temperature-controlled cabinets were used to grow ginseng cell cultures.

We should continue to study the effects of space flight on botanical objects, but also protect the planet's unique treasures here on Earth. We may yet learn the full medical properties of the Root of Life, the miraculous *jen shen*.

Chapter 2

Mysteries of the Lost Amber Room

THE YEAR 2005 marked the sixtieth anniversary of the Allied victory over Nazi Germany. The generation that fought World War II is now fading from the scene, but many questions from that time remain to be answered. One of these concerns the whereabouts of Russia's greatest lost treasure: the Amber Room of Frederick I. This priceless work of decorative art was stolen from Russia by the Nazis and taken to the city of Königsberg, from which it vanished in the waning days of the war.

The Setting

Königsberg (later Kaliningrad) is an ice-free port city situated on the Baltic Sea coast, the farthest western corner of modern Russia. It was founded by the Teutonic knights when they spread eastward during the thirteenth century.

Ever since its foundation, Königsberg has been a city of paradoxes and enigmas. The knights originally planned to build the city some two hundred kilometers to the east, at the Neman River. During their rest stop at a mountain that contained a heathen place of worship, the knights observed a solar eclipse. The Teutonic Order's Magisters considered the phenomenon to be a sign from God, and decided not to disobey it. The mountain later became known as Königs Berg, or Royal Mountain.

Königsberg Castle— original site of the Amber Room.

In 1255 the main castle of Königsberg was founded on the bank of the Pregel River. A ring of fifteen fortresses (allegedly united by a system of underground tunnels) surrounds the city.

Formerly the capital of the dukes of Prussia and later the capital of East Prussia, Königsberg was ceded to the Soviet Union in 1945 under the Potsdam agreement. The city's strategic importance was all too apparent to Stalin. In June 1941 it had been used by the Germans as a staging ground for one of the main assaults against Soviet Russia, and it remained a very important naval base for the duration of the war. Over one hundred thousand Soviet soldiers lost their lives in the operation to take the city from the Germans.

In 1946 the Königsberg area was sealed off from the rest of the Soviet Union. Renamed Kaliningrad, it became a vital military outpost. An ugly House of Soviets replaced the ruins of Königsberg Castle in the center of the city.

When the city was part of the Nazi Reich, it was under the control of the murderous Erich Koch. Koch treated the city's people with great cruelty as he carried out Hitler's plans. After the war, Koch hid from justice under

Erich Koch.

a false name. In 1959 he was found and sentenced to death. Due to his poor health he was kept in prison until he died in 1986. Koch took a number of secrets to his grave.

Among Koch's last statements was the assertion, "Where lies my treasure, there also lies the Amber Room."

The Amber Room

Yantarnaya komnata (the Amber Room) was built as Frederick I's study at Königsberg Castle in 1711. Five years later, it was given as a present to Peter the Great to commemorate Prussia's alliance with Russia. It was later installed in the palace of Catherine the Great at Tsarskoye Selo, the opulent summer residence of the Russian royal family just outside St. Petersburg (later Leningrad).

The Amber Room's decorations covered eighteen hundred square feet and consisted of handcrafted panels made of six tons of amber (the lightest gem in the world) and Italian mosaics decorated with diamonds, emeralds, and rubies. It is often referred to as the Eighth Wonder of the World. People believed that it possessed magical energy. There is a belief in the Baltics that amber ("northern gold" and "sun-drenched stone") has miraculous healing powers.

When the German armies besieged Leningrad during the Second World War, they dismantled the famous Amber Room. (The desperate Soviets attempted to hide the Amber Room by wallpapering over it.) Soon after the Amber Room was seized, the Nazis sent it west by train. It was taken back to Königsberg Castle and displayed in one of the halls of the Königsberg

Museum.

Just before the capitulation of the city in 1945, the Germans once again dismantled the room and packed it in crates, intending to ship it back to Berlin. It has never been seen since. The hunt for the collection of jewel-encrusted panels that make up the Amber Room has been a great post-war quest. For five decades the KGB, the Stasi (East German secret police), and unknown others have failed in the search.

Frederick I of Prussia.

Lethal Treasures

Vera Bruyussova, widow of a noted Soviet archaeologist charged to look for the treasure, revealed that her husband, Alexander, wrote a memo to the Soviet leadership in 1955 stating: "I do not believe that the treasure is lost."

There have been many speculations as to what had happened to it, and some people are convinced that the diligent quest has brought death and misfortune to those involved (the so-called Curse of the Amber Room).

A Soviet team charged with finding the Amber Room secretly petitioned Moscow in 1984, asking why they was prevented from freely investigating the fate of the room without interference from the Soviet military and KGB.

A general of Russian intelligence named Gusev reportedly died in a mysterious automobile accident after he talked to a newspaper reporter about the Amber Room. Very little is known about this incident.

Some believe the Amber Room perished in a fire when a Soviet bomb hit the Königsberg castle in the 1945 Red Army offensive. Leonid Arinshtein, a World War II veteran and an advisor to the Russian Culture Fund president, believes Königsberg was set on fire before the city was captured. The castle started burning on the second or third day after the city had been captured. A German caretaker who was there on April 8 told Arinshtein that the Amber Room's panels, packed in boxes, were kept in the basement of the castle.

The Red Army had no reason to set its country's newly recovered treasures on fire. That means some other force, perhaps a Nazi underground group, an agile, deadly, and swift underground force, was carrying out the orders of the Reich. The Red Army was engaged in a fierce, deadly battle to capture a city protected by the complex fortress system and did not control the situation yet. The fire was spreading from the outskirts to the center of the city, Soviet troops were exhausted after months-old battles in Prussia, German forces were fighting in the port area, and almost all of the population was evacuated. Entire neighborhoods were burning and chaos reigned.

If some unknown group has been concealing knowledge of the Amber Room's location, its operatives have been quite effective.

A Deadly Quest

Mysterious deaths attributed to the knowledge about the room include that of Dr. Alfred Rohde. Rohde was in control of the Amber Room as the director of the Königsberg museum under the Nazi regime. He and his wife died from typhoid the day before their scheduled interrogation by NKVD (the KGB of the period). Soviet intelligence officers did not find bodies of the deceased couple. Apparently, they opened the tomb in early 1946, but it was empty. Just recently it was learned, from an interview with Russian naval archaeologists (Königsberg, October 31, 2003), that Dr. Rohde had been able to escape from Soviet control for several days and probably left Königsberg to check something outside the city. He later returned, only to die...or vanish forever. Russian researchers believe he visited the Pillau Castle (formerly a German submarine base).

Another strange disappearance was that of the doctor who signed the death certificates of the Rohdes. Then there was Georg Stein, the relentless investigator of the Amber Room's whereabouts. He was found dead and naked in the middle of a forest in Germany, his stomach ripped apart by a scalpel.

Stein was a German researcher who helped to deliver to the Soviets hundreds of displaced "cultural valuables" (Nazi-looted treasures). But the Soviets would not allow him enter the forbidden Kaliningrad region, although he sent them thousands of pages of archives, according to Avenir Ovsyanov, who continues the quest.

Ovsyanov was once a military engineering student. Under orders of his superiors he and his classmates blew up the ruins of Königsberg Castle. He was a young soldier then and is not at all happy now about his involvement. In an interview to *Izvestiya* in 2003 he stated that the ruined castle was finally demolished in 1968.

Soviet Investigations

Ovsyanov, now chief of the Department for Search for Cultural Valuables of the Kaliningrad region, revealed several interesting details in 2002.

In the summer of 1945, a special Soviet team headed by T. L. Beljayeva, was sent to Königsberg. Beljayeva's group found Russian valuables looted by Nazis, including libraries, monographs, crowns, paintings, and archaeological collections. Apparently, some of these came from Tsarskoye Selo.

A team sent by the Committee for Arts of the USSR was also operating in the area, collecting Nazi-looted antiques. Sixty crates of cultural valuables collected by the Beljayeva group remained in Königsberg, but no one knows what happened to them. The best sources are diaries and private letters.

Other recovered cultural valuables were ultimately "withdrawn" by operatives of the NKVD or KGB. It would be interesting to find out about the Soviet intelligence agents who had worked in Nazi-controlled Königsberg, but the KGB files have been out of reach of even Russian researchers.

In 1967 the Soviet government created a special commission to search for the Amber Room and other museum valuables. It was headquartered in Moscow, and its arm in the Baltics was the Kaliningrad archaeological expedition (KGAE). This group was denied access to many top-secret areas, and was hampered by bureaucracy. The KGAE was itself a secret group and as such, its work was classified. Yet even this group was denied access to the secret archives concerning looted Soviet treasures. According to Ovsyanov, the archives still remain closed, although the Soviet Union is no more. The KGAE was disbanded in 1983.

The nefarious East German Stasi also spent years trying to find the Amber Room. This organization's efforts included the creation of a special unit that functioned during the 1970s and '80s.

The Quest Continues

A former Soviet architect of Kaliningrad named Maximov recalled that when the Soviets captured the city they found a freshly flooded well in a western wing of the castle. It sloped downward to great depths. Some believe that this is where the Amber Room was hidden. Russian and German archaeologists who explored the basements of the castle found ancient weapons and jewelry.

However, Ovsyanov points out that prior to the final destruction of the castle in 1968, the basements surely were visited because they were easily accessible.

Another possible location of the Amber Room may be the subterranean vaults of the old Pillau (Baltiysk) castle. It is quite possible that Dr. Rohde came there when he slipped from the grasp of the NKVD. Pillau, the main base of the Russian Baltic Navy, is located west of Kaliningrad. The castle vaults were sealed off in the 1940s, after the Soviets learned that German troops had filled the area with explosives and mines.

The Nazis used the castle as military headquarters for the defense of Pillau. When Red Army troops entered the castle, not a single German officer was found. They had used secret passageways to escape the fortress. The area was then used as a top-secret Soviet Naval base.

Did the Amber Room escape on board the German liner *Wilhelm Gustloff* only to be torpedoed in the Baltic by an enemy submarine? Russian archaeologists believe that Nazis would not have risked transporting precious art objects through the dangerous waters of the Baltic Sea where Soviet submarines lay in waiting. There are speculations that the Amber Room is hidden on the shores of the Baltic Sea. Recent finds in the area support such assumption.

International treasure hunters have searched endlessly for the Amber Room, digging up cellars and salt mines, scouring churches and caves. They've looked in Austria, Germany, Poland, Lithuania, and the Czech Republic. Some believe that the Amber Room may still be hidden somewhere in half-flooded caves under Kaliningrad. Several divers have lost their lives trying to find out if the Nazis buried the Amber Room there.

Hans Stadelman, a steadfast German researcher, believes the Nazis hid the panels below a building in the town of Weimar.

On beaches of the Kaliningrad region one can collect fragments of natural amber thrown out by waves of the Baltic Sea. But the sea and its shores have hid their secrets well.

In 1997, German police found one of the Amber Room's mosaics. The son of a former German officer, who had accompanied the Amber Room on its way to Königsberg during the war, was trying to sell the piece through his lawyer. It was a panel measuring 55 by 70.5 centimeters, depicting two couples lounging in a garden with their dogs. Apparently, the seller's father was a truck driver for the German Army who took the panel in 1941 as his convoy was bombed. After the recovery the panel was returned to Russia.

The city of paradoxes may face its evils again. East European criminals who engage in contraband, white slavery, and drug smuggling use Kaliningrad for their transit needs. The old Gestapo building is used by the Russian secret police (the FSB). There have been increased neo-Nazi activities in Kaliningrad, by Germans and by ethnic Russian supporters of fascist and nationalistic movements. Erich Koch would have been proud.

Chapter 3

Secrets of the Emperor's Lost Tomb

A REPORT PUBLISHED in the *China Daily* newspaper on Friday, December 13, 2002, attracted my attention. I, too, had researched unsolved mysteries of Shihuangdi (or Ying Zheng), a very remarkable Chinese ruler who lived a life of danger over two thousand years ago. This research began over thirty years ago, when I, a Soviet teenager at the time, read about an ancient Chinese mirror used to diagnose illnesses. Like many of my peers, I was interested in what we call in Russian *zagadki istorii,* or enigmas of history. And what a fascinating enigma the life of Emperor Shihuangdi turned out to be! But let us start with the article in the Chinese newspaper, and go step by step.

Mysterious Mausoleum

The article was titled "Survey to Solve Tomb Mystery." According to its author, Chinese scientists would use remote sensing and geophysical techniques to investigate the mysterious mausoleum of the first Qin (pronounced

"Chin") emperor.

The grand mausoleum is located thirty-six kilometers east of Xi'an, capital of northwest China's Shaanxi Province. It was the eternal resting place for Shighuangdi, the emperor of the Qin Dynasty (221–206 B.C.) who unified China for the first time in its turbulent history. The mausoleum was a creation mixed with the blood and tears of many people.

Its construction started in 247 B.C. Chinese historical records stated that it took seven hudred thousand people thirty-six years to build the luxurious underground tomb. The mausoleum occupies about 56.25 square kilometers. Exotic treasures from all over the land and concubines were buried with the deceased emperor. The mausoleum was an elaborate construction, with jewels on the ceiling representing the constellations. Mercury was used to create imitations of the Yellow River and the Yangtze, lakes and the seas, assembled in such a way that they seemed to flow. Those who built the underground tomb were executed or walled inside the mausoleum, lest they spread stories about its gold, gems, and secrets.

The actual structure and position of the mausoleum are still a mystery, despite the fact that several surveys having been conducted since the 1970s. According to Guan Haiyan, director of the Shaanxi Remote Sensing Center, Chinese scientists and archaeologists are presently carrying out a large-scale investigation of the tomb. Guan Haiyan is also the project's senior engineer. He revealed that the scientists would use aerial remote sensing and geophysical techniques to identify the position, depth, and basic structure of the underground palace, as well as the sixty-square-kilometer area surrounding the tomb. Reading the article, I got the impression that the Chinese government is very much interested in finding out about the secrets the mausoleum may hold. The survey, listed as a key project of the National High Technology Research and Development Program of the People's Republic of China, is by far the most comprehensive research ever on the mausoleum. In December 1987, the United Nations Educational, Scientific, and Cultural Organization listed the mausoleum as a World

Emperor Shihuangdi.

Heritage Site, together with the Great Wall and the Imperial Palace of the Ming and Qing dynasties.

Were there truly rivers and lakes of mercury underground? What other secrets are buried in the Shaanxi Province?

Bing Ma Yong

Meanwhile, the discoveries already made at the site have aroused great interest throughout the world. Back in 1974 near Xi'an, a group of Chinese farmers from the Yen Tsai commune in Lintong County were digging a well and found, in the process, several terra-cotta figures buried deep underground. Future investigations uncovered burial pits of terra-cotta warriors and horses. Three vaults containing thousands of figures (known as *bing ma yong*) were found 1.5 kilometers east of the mausoleum, and two sets of large bronze chariots and horses were excavated west of it. Seven thousand life-sized terra-cotta warriors, very detailed and painted like the soldiers of the Qin Empire, seem to guard many secrets of their dead emperor.

They represented chariot warriors, clay archers, infantry, and cavalrymen. The terra-cotta warriors were armed with real weapons. Each warrior was exquisitely and very accurately built and possessed unique features.

At the time of Shihuangdi's death, the Qin Empire stopped burying living human beings for some time. The terra-cotta soldiers would be replacement for the old funeral burial. But the emperor's son Huhai, according to ancient records, had ordered that all Shihuangdi's concubines who had never borne children be buried inside Shihuangdi's tomb. To prevent the builders of the tombs from revealing the inside of the tomb, Huhai also sealed it with the builders inside. The tomb, decorated with precious stones and gems, was said to have traps, crossbows, and automatic arrows to eliminate potential grave robbers. Also, there were eternal lamps, lit by oil refined from mermaid fish from the East China Sea. A Chinese book from the fifth century B.C. mentioned that moonlight pearls suspended in the tumulus lit both day and night.

In 1979, the Museum of Qin Shihuangdi was established in China. Visitors to the country have the opportunity to see the terra-cotta warriors of the emperor's long-ago buried army.

The discovery of the buried legion has created a stir all over the world, but according to the article in *China Daily*, this is just the tip of the iceberg.

As opposed to the Egyptian pyramids, which were constructed above ground level, the mausoleum is a huge underground complex designed to mirror the street plan of the Qin Dynasty's capital. It is the first and the largest imperial mausoleum in China.

Tens of thousands of statues and treasures undoubtedly still remain to be unearthed from the site. Chinese archaeologists believe that these finds will be extremely valuable to study the Qin Dynasty's society. What would the discovery of the crystal diagnosis device do to our medicine? What if the archaeologists find the legendary eternal lamps of the emperor's tomb?

A Handful of History

Shihuangdi was probably the most influential of the three hundred emperors who ruled royal dynasties throughout Chinese history. He established China's first feudal empire, the first unified empire in the history of China. He was born in Handan, an ancient town in northern China. According to ancient legends, he was inside his mother's womb for twelve months. The future emperor was said to possess a high-bridged nose, elongated eyes, and a "leopard" voice. His life was unusual, and his name is well known to the Chinese people, for he played an important part in their history. And yet, we still know little about him. I have collected information about him for a number of years, mainly because of the amazing mirror he supposedly possessed. I used many sources, including the records of the grand historian Sima Qian of the Han court. He had a great habit of collecting historical material during his travels on imperial service, and he had excellent access to the imperial library.

The terra-cotta warriors of Shihuangdi.

Shihuangdi was crowned at the age of thirteen. Twenty-five years later he unified China through a series of wars. Who was he?

His childhood was less than happy, and very unstable. The seven states of China were warring among themselves, and the blood of China's people inundated its cities and villages. Yi Ren, the boys' father, was a hostage in the Principality of Zhao. But the court gossip had it that his real father was Lü Buwei, Qin's future prime minister.

Lü was a wealthy merchant doing business in Zhao, but foremost a keen political observer, who recognized the potential of Zhuangxiangwang (Yi Ren). Lü Buwei invested in him and also gave him a favorite concubine as a present. In 259 B.C., King Zhaoxiangwang died and Xiaowenwang ascended to the throne of Qin. (The name "China" most likely originated in the Qin Dynasty.) Lü Buwei was responsible for making Zhuangxiangwang an adopted son of the Qin king. Not long after becoming the king, Zhuangxiangwang dispatched his warrior prime minister Lü Buwei against the Zhou kingdom to crush a conspiracy of local nobles to restrict Qin's expansion. Zhou was no more. Then a series of wars ensued against Haan, Wei, and Zhao Principalities. But later the Qin forces suffered a defeat at the hands of the united Yan-Zhao-Haan-Chu-Wei armies.

In May of 246 B.C. Zhuangxiangwang died, and Shihuangdi became ruler of Qin. In reality, however, Lü Buwei and his former concubine, now empress dowager, controlled the country. After Shihuangdi became the King of Qin, Lü Buwei served him as prime minister, and together with other worthy nobles was responsible for all political and military matters of Qin court for the next thirteen years.

The young king wanted to create a powerful and united kingdom, and sought capable people to assist him.

Zhong Fu, or "Uncle-Father," was the name Shihuangdi used to refer to Lü Buwei (a proxy, or second father was the proper meaning). By then Lü Buwei had supplied the queen mother with a new lover, and she bore him two sons, who were the king's half-brothers. Shihuangdi ordered them killed after he learned of their existence. Their father, mandarin Changxin-hou, rebelled in 238 B.C. against the king and was defeated. His two sons (the king's half brothers) were killed and their bodies were thrown on the ground in bags. The empress dowager was banished to a fortress away from her son.

Lü Buwei lost his power, prestige, and position. In 235 B.C., he died after drinking poison.

The emperor did forgive his mother later and brought her back from exile.

How China Was Unified

The actual process of unification of the huge country through military campaigns and conquest was started in 473 B.C. The Qin state was isolated in the west of China by a section of the Yellow River and a mountain range, and thus protected from invasion by other Chinese armies. At the same time, its military forces gained experience protecting the borders against foreign invaders. During the tumultuous Warring States period, the northern and western Chinese states of Qin, Zhao, and Yen had all to defend their borders by building fortified walls to prevent an invasion by Xiongnu (nomads). This fortified defense line became known as the Great Wall centuries later when the iron hand of the future emperor connected the fragmented walls through the hard labor of thousands of prisoners. The wall took ten years to build at the rate of around mile a day for the total of three thousand miles.

Shihuangdi basically continued the process, and did so very skillfully, using military force, brutality, and very cunning diplomacy. Qin became the strongest of the seven states, and after the other six were finally defeated, China became a unified empire, a feudal monarchy under a strong central bureaucratic government. All military and administrative powers of China were concentrated in the hands of the emperor, who ruled his country through twelve ministries directly responsible to him.

He had a good advisor in the person of a keen observer and psychologist named Li Si (Li Szu), who came from a humble background. The emperor had gathered other capable people around him: a strategist named Liao and an irrigation expert named Zhengguo. He carried on his military conquest with determination and cruelty, year after year full of bloody battles. For instance, in a number of battles against Pingyang of Zhao (234 B.C.), the emperor's forces killed over one hundred thousand enemy soldiers. The conquest was accompanied by intrigues, treachery, and earthquakes. In 240 B.C. a strange comet was seen in the sky.

Finally, by 221 B.C., Shihuangdi, during the twenty-sixth year of his reign, completed the unification of China. He established the so-called Jun-Xian System; that is, the prefecture system. He listened to Li-Si, his prime minister, and established thirty-six so-called prefectures or commandaries (administrative areas, something like our states) broken down further into counties, townships, rings, and lis.

The same prime minister advised Shihuangdi to assume the title of emperor, and the king did so. (He used the ancient word for emperor, *huangdi.*) He was now more than a mere king; he was the august emperor of a nation unified by sword and blood. He was the first emperor, and his realm and dynasty, according to his plans, were to last thousands of years.

The Emperor's Deeds and Misdeeds

The emperor believed in and promoted balance and order throughout his empire.

His monetary policy included abolishing the currencies of the defeated states and establishing Qin coinage as the main currency of the land. Then the emperor introduced the official script of Qin throughout China and thus unified the written Chinese language. He also standardized weights and measures in China.

Besides his great and bloody military conquest to unify China, he was known for other momentous projects: paving the straight highways (*zhi dao*) across the country, building and linking the Great Wall, digging of numerous canals to link up the water system, paving a road to Inner Mongolia, creating a great southern highway, and building the exclusively imperial roads. He conducted military campaigns against the Huns and populated the newly created administrative units with convicts and slaves from other areas of China. But the emperor also moved and resettled a number of wealthy Chinese to develop the city of Xianyang. As one of his reforms, Shihuangdi abolished aristocracy. The new emperor believed in meritocracy; personal abilities made someone a leader, not hereditary titles.

In his campaigns throughout China and northern Vietnam, the emperor relocated hundreds of thousands of people from various areas to the south of China.

The emperor believed in arms control: his subordinates collected and confiscated weapons from all over China and melted them into huge stat-

The Great Wall of China.

ues. There were twelve of those bronze statues; curiously, they were made to resemble strange, giant humanoid creatures sighted in 221 B.C. in Lingtiao. He also personally inspected his realm on many occasions; he climbed mountains and organized expeditions to foreign lands to look for medical cures.

Apparently Shihuangdi, who believed that he possessed god-like powers, was also interested in alchemy. He was looking for a long and healthy life, or better yet, immortality. He sent expeditions on sea voyages abroad to find the secret. Yet Shihuangdi also knew that death might be coming and ordered the construction of his tomb early in his reign.

Li-Si was a powerful proponent of Legalism, a school of philosophy on how to run a state efficiently and ruthlessly, placing the welfare of the state above individuals and morals. It was the complete opposite of Confucianism, the very foundation of Chinese society. In 213 B.C. the emperor outlawed the Confucian schools of thought and ordered the burning of their books. Hundreds of Confucians were burned alive as well. Others throughout China were stoned to death. Shihuangdi exercised thought control by burning ancient manuscripts, various historical records, and works of Asian classics, which were forever destroyed. But he excluded books on medicine, divination, and agriculture. Those who questioned his policies generally faced capital punishment, along with their relatives. A lesser punishment would be years of hard labor: connecting smaller, existing sections of the Great Wall of China and building huge stretches of roads to connect the empire. Philosophical debates were outlawed. Heretical scholars mixed with criminals and peasants. Tyranny and oppression were the hallmarks of this short-lived dynasty.

Little wonder that China's first peasant uprising took place in 209 B.C., after the emperor died.

Thus, Shihuangdi was a great Chinese emperor, an ambitious nation-builder, a cruel conqueror, a brutal and fearsome tyrant, and a seeker of knowledge.

The death of the emperor has an odd history of its own. Shihuangdi was just fifty years old when died from a sudden illness in 210 B.C., during a state inspection visit to one of the eastern prefectures. His trusted prime minister Li Si and a court official decided to hide the fact of the death from everyone until his will could be changed. They covered his decaying body with salt to disguise his death, while helping his eighteenth son Huhai ascend to the throne through bloodshed and intrigues. After becoming the ruler of his late father's empire, Huhai made sure his half-brothers and half-sisters were killed so no challenge to his rule would arise anywhere in the land.

The dynasty did not last. It was all over for the Qin Empire in 206 B.C., when its last emperor, Zi Ying, was killed in a bloody conflict and struggle for power. The old, wise prime minister was cruelly murdered, too, betrayed by his former co-conspirator Zhao Gao. Massacres, chaos, mayhem, the rule of criminal gangs and rebels, betrayals, and bloodshed ensued. The royal palaces were looted and burned. Soldiers were sent to dig up the Emperor

Shihuangdi's tomb in the Lishan Mountains. We do not know what they removed from the tomb, and how they damaged it. In 202 B.C., after a four-year war between the rebel armies, the Han dynasty was established, and relative peace returned to the weary country.

The Magic Mirror and Other Mysteries of the First Emperor

Many years ago, while a teenager in the Soviet Union, I read a wonderful novel, *Tais of Athens,* written by the superb Soviet scientist, explorer, writer, and freethinker Ivan Efremov. He was an enigmatic person who had a life full of adventure and scientific discoveries, and he clearly possessed knowledge of the secrets of antiquity from India, China, Crete, and other places. Where, for instance, did he find such intriguing information about the ancient Chinese mirror, featured in *Tais of Athens,* that basically was an x-ray machine used to diagnose disease? Years later, and after my own extensive research, I found more about the mirror, but Efremov knew about it back in the 1960s or even earlier.

Several sources refer to a "magic mirror" in ancient China that could illuminate the insides, organs, and bones of the human body. This amazing device was obviously used to diagnose illnesses. This ancient X-ray machine illuminated the bones and organs of a patient's body, giving a reversed image of it. And this magic mirror, or an x-ray machine of antiquity, belonged to Shihuangdi.

The emperor looked for immortality, and sent out expeditions of young children and teenagers, under the command of Xu Fudong, to seek the fountain of youth.

Reportedly, Xu Fudong actually landed in Japan in 219 B.C. and stayed there; when his crew grew up, they populated the island nation.

Ginseng, the vitamin-rich herb, increases the body's resistance to infections and is an effective treatment for cancer and exposure to toxic substances; it is an ancient herb that is believed to prevent cancer, heal infections, and cure impotence. Ancient Chinese legends tell the story of Shihuangdi's failed quest for ginseng in the Far East taiga. According to the story, the emperor in 200 B.C. dispatched six thousand of his best soldiers to harvest the herb, but the entire expedition mysteriously disappeared.

The *Yih King* (Book of Changes)

W. H. Allen & Co. published *Mythical Monsters* by Charles Gould in London in 1886. Gould discussed mythical creatures and attempted to demonstrate that some legendary animals do indeed exist. The author's main emphasis was on the creatures that populated the ancient folklore of China: dragons, sea serpents, and the Chinese phoenix.

An ancient Chinese book of mysterious origins, the *Yih King* or *I Ching*, is mentioned by Gould in quotations from a comprehensive Chinese encyclopedia, the *Yuen Klei Lei Han,* completed in A.D. 1710. The *Yih King* contained information about dragons and other very curious matters, whose meaning was not clear to most Chinese—or possibly just to those who did not possess the necessary training. This book escaped the mass burning of Chinese historical books and records ordered by Shihuangdi in 213 B.C. According to the French researcher Monsieur de la Couperie in the *Journal of the Royal Asiatic Society,* the *Yih King* is the oldest of the Chinese classics and a mysterious book that requires prolonged attention to make it reveal its secrets.

Those Chinese who had studied in Europe in the nineteenth century and who knew the *Yih King* claimed that information about electricity, steam power, astronomical laws, the spherical nature of the Earth, and many other sciences and matters were contained in the ancient book. There were secrets that the Chinese scholars hoped to unveil after applying a thorough knowledge of modern sciences to the study of the classics. Gould, however, refused to accept the idea that there could be a possible connection "between their rude notions and our sciences."

"It is not a mysterious book of fates and prognostics," wrote Gould, "but a valuable collection of documents of old antiquity."

Perhaps Shihuangdi, who made sure the mysterious book was not burned with other collections as his atrocious policies demanded, knew how to read the book and unveil the secrets contained on its pages. Perhaps his magic mirror and the eternal illumination of the tomb were some of the secrets.

What was the importance of the *Book of Changes* to Shihuangdi?

The *Yih King* may be one the oldest sacred texts in the world. It is one of the greatest treasures of wisdom on Earth. It is a most obscure, complex, and mysterious work of mental and moral philosophy and divination.

The book was written around 2850 B.C. It is the most widely read of the five Chinese Classics. The book has been of great interest to many people. One of them was dispatched to the Orient by Louis XIV of France.

Jean-Baptiste Regis was a Jesuit who was sent to China in 1698 at the age of thirty-five on a mission to study science and religion. He spent close to forty years in the Orient and was instrumental in preparing the general map of China. Chinese Emperor K'ang-hi (1662–1722) was quite friendly to the Jesuits, and a number of important Chinese books and sources were open to them. Regis was one of a number of French Jesuits in the country sent by Louis XIV to engage in astronomical observations and Chinese geographical, cartographical, and topographical research. They had received special training from scientists at the Paris Observatory and used state-of-the art instruments. The Jesuits made a number of scientific expeditions throughout China, Tibet, Mongolia, Siberia, and Manchuria. They measured the Great Wall and made excellent maps. Those who knew China well regarded their map of China to be a masterpiece. But what is important here is that Regis appreciated ancient Chinese books and translated the *Yih King*. Julius Mol, in Stuttgart, edited the translation in 1864. The first volume contained "Prologomena," a valuable and fascinating introduction to the classics of China.

Regis died in Beijing in 1738. He played the most active role in making the map of China, a land that was still a mystery to Europeans in the eighteenth century. We really do not know what he learned in the *Yih King* or how much it helped him in his endeavors on behalf of his order and Louis XIV.

I suspect the knowledge gained by Jean-Baptiste Regis is not lost, but guarded.

In pre-dynastic times, the mythical Five Emperors (Wu Ti) ruled China. The Five Emperors ruled in succession during the "golden age of antiquity" (prior to 2357 B.C.) and have usually been considered sages and cultural heroes, if not semi-divine beings. Hence we find that these Five Emperors, Fu Hsi (One Who Subdues Animals), Shen Nung (the Divine Farmer), Huang-Ti (the Yellow Emperor), Shao Hao, and Chuan Hsu, have each been credited with many inventions as long ago as five thousand years. In August of 2001, FATE magazine published my article about the Yellow Emperor, a legendary giver of knowledge. The author of the *Yih King* is the legendary Chinese Emperor Fu Hsi (2953–2838 B.C.).

What wonderful discoveries are in store for Chinese archaeologists when they survey the mysterious mausoleum of the first Qin emperor?

Chapter 4

Subudai Bagatur and Enigmas of the Mongol Empire

THESE ARE FOUR HOUNDS of my Temudjin, reared on human flesh; he tied them to an iron chain; these hounds have copper foreheads, carved teeth, thorn-like tongues, and iron hearts. Instead of a horse lash they use crooked sabers. They drink dew, and ride the wind; in battles they devour human flesh. Now they have been unchained from their chain; they salivate; they are merry. The four hounds are: Jebe, Khubilai, Jelme, and Subudai."

This is what Jamukha, the stepbrother (*anda*) of Genghis Khan, said of the bloody Universal Ruler and his fellow fighters. Jamukha, a relative and clan chief, helped Temudjin free his family when they were kidnapped. Years later the "hounds" captured Jamukha, who rebelled against Genghis Khan, and they murdered him. When they captured Jamukha, Genghis Khan did Jamukha the honor of killing him by rolling him up in a carpet and crushing him with boulders, so that the blood would remain in the body. In the years that followed, the hounds killed millions of people throughout the world and crushed thriving civilizations. Their conquest was a terrible disaster of the Middle Ages.

The Mongols of the thirteenth century laid waste to nations, cities, towns, and villages. They destroyed, burned, pillaged, raped, and killed. Their cruelty was but a part of the comprehensive strategy of conquest. The Mongols instilled fear and sought to convince the world that resistance was futile. They made sure that tales of their savagery and merciless slaughter preceded them wherever they went.

A Cart Unlike Any Other

The Mongols carried their tents on four-wheeled carts, and they also used two-wheeled carts covered with black felt thoroughly treated with tallow to waterproof it. Usually camels, horses, or oxen drew such carts. The vehicles provided them with enhanced mobility, for the Mongols carried their families, belongings, supplies, and provisions therein.

Ancient Mongol records tell that Subudai Bagatur, one of the "hounds," had a habit of resting in a special vehicle during his military campaigns. This vehicle was made of a special metal, and no arrow could penetrate its sides. Not long ago, according to Viktor Nikitin in *Tayni inikh mirov* (Saint Petersburg, 2001), a two-wheeled, metal-covered vehicle was unearthed during archaeological excavations in the vicinity of Pusan, South Korea. A chemical analysis of the metal indicated that it was alloyed steel, with an admixture of molybdenum and tungsten. A bullet could not penetrate sheathing made from this metal.

My inquiries about this vehicle to archaeologists in South Korea and others in the United States who study Korean archaeology received no replies, and I have not been able to ascertain the veracity of the Russian author's report.

Could nomadic tribes from the Asian steppes have built such a vehicle?

Metallurgy is the process of working ores into artifacts. Mongol warriors were not metallurgists. The conquerors from the steppes borrowed technology from the conquered nations, from the Chinese, Arabs, and Persians. Their armies were accompanied by wise and learned foreigners, as well as forcefully conscripted soldiers from among the vanquished people. Still, the Mongols could not have created such an alloy.

Tungsten and Molybdenum

Let us look at the metals that were admixed into the alloy.

Molybdenum, a silvery-white metal, was discovered in 1778. It is used in alloys, electrodes, and catalysts. A well-known Nazi artillery piece, "Big Bertha," contained molybdenum as an essential component of its steel. Native molybdenum does not occur; the metal is obtained principally from molybdenite. To get pure samples, metallurgists first dissolve the oxide in ammonium hydroxide to make ammonium molybdate and afterward reduce the molybdate with hydrogen. In its pure state, molybdenum is somewhat heavier than iron, but melts at a much higher temperature—4,730 degrees Fahrenheit as compared to 2,795 degrees.

The word *tungsten* is Swedish for "heavy stone." China is reported to have about seventy-five percent of the world's tungsten resources. Tungsten has the highest melting point and lowest vapor pressure of all metals, and at temperatures of more than three thousand degrees Fahrenheit has the highest tensile strength. Tungsten has excellent corrosion resistance and is attacked only slightly by most mineral acids. Tungsten compounds are used for cutting tools and high-temperature lubricants.

The first attempts to produce tungsten steel were made in 1855, but industrial use was not possible because of the high price of tungsten. Tungsten occurs in the natural state only in the form of chemical compounds with other elements and is usually mined underground. The ore is first crushed and milled to liberate the tungsten mineral crystals.

Most of the tungsten metal powder is converted to tungsten carbide by reaction with pure carbon powder at 1,650 to 4,000 degrees Fahrenheit in

pusher or batch furnaces, a process called carburization. Tungsten carbide is, quantitatively, the most important tungsten compound. Because of its hardness, it is the main constituent in cemented carbide. Hard metal is the most important use of tungsten. Its main constituent is tungsten monocarbide (WC), with a hardness close to diamond.

The most promising area of growth for tungsten demand in the military arena is in the manufacture of armor-piercing projectiles, particularly for small-caliber ammunition.

Mongolia was a horse-based culture, and the Mongolian steppes and deserts were not centers of advanced metallurgy.

How did nomadic warriors of the thirteenth century obtain this vehicle?

Fame Measured in Blood

In the thirteenth century, Mongolia was one of the most powerful states in the world. A capable Mongol warrior and chieftain called Temudjin Esukhei gathered various scattered nomadic tribes under his leadership, named his state Mongolia, and renamed himself Genghis Khan (also spelled Chingghis or Jenghiz Khan). The difficult and bloody process of establishing the nomadic state was described in the famous Mongolian document *Nuuts tovchoo* (Secret history of the Mongols).

Mongolian yurts and wagons.

Temudjin, one of the most famous conquerors of history, extended his empire across Asia to the Adriatic Sea. He died on August 18, 1227. A warrior and ruler who started from obscure and insignificant beginnings, Genghis Khan used the military prowess of his united tribes to create a nation that spanned from China to Turkey and Iraq, from Egypt to Russia, all the way over to Korea and down to Vietnam.

The Mongols were known as Tartars in Europe. Their warlords, cruel but brilliant military leaders, created the largest empire known to man. The Mongol war machine is the basis for every military in the world today. Of all the commanders who arrived from Mongolia, Subudai Bagatur was the greatest. He led the western onslaught of the Mongol army against Russia, Europe, and the Caucasian countries.

Subudai outlived Genghis Khan and continued to serve his people under Batu Khan and Ugedey, the second son of Genghis Khan.

Mongol Conquests

Genghis Khan conquered the northeastern part of China in the years 1211 through 1215. Subudai and another trusted general, Chupe Noyon, each with a battalion-size military unit, terrorized the Chinese countryside, cleverly using the rich technology of the Chinese empire against them. Then the Mongol leader marched against Central Asia, launching an offensive on Muhammad, Shah of Khorezm (1200–1220). The detachment of the Mongol army, led by Jebe and Subudai, the same detachment that had made war on Muhammad and his son Jalal-ad-Din (1200–1231), attacked the kingdom of Georgia several times in the early 1220s.

In 1221, a reconnaissance detachment of fifteen thousand Mongols separated from the Central Asian expedition and traveled around the Caspian Sea, exploring the lands on its western shore. It was Subudai (and Jebe) who led the Mongol horsemen when they met with a superior Russian force and their Kipchak Cuman (Polovtsy) allies. The Mongol light cavalry outmaneuvered the Russian forces and defeated them in the battle of the Kalka (1223). Russia was conquered in 1237 and 1238. Batu Khan sent Subudai to quell a revolt led by Jiku and Baian in 1238 and 1239. Next, Subudai's forces descended upon the Ukrainian steppe, conquering Polovtsy in 1239 and Kiev in 1240.

Later, Subudai set his sights on Europe. Hungary attracted the Mongols because of its wide-open steppes. In 1241 the Mongol invaders charged into central Europe and defeated the combined armies of Germany, Poland, and Bohemia in the battle of Liegnitz. Other parts of Subudai's force descended into Hungary from the Carpathian Mountains from several directions. The Hungarian king fled, and the Mongols conquered the country, establishing garrisons to enforce their control.

Only the news of the death in Mongolia of the Great Khan Ugedey saved Western Europe from Subudai Bagatur and his merciless, disciplined, fearless Mongol hordes. In 1242, the Mongols departed back to Asia.

Mongols Invade Korea

Korea is an ancient country with a history of more than five thousand s.

But it experienced many bloody periods, and Mongol invaders caused one of them.

In 1231, the Mongols invaded Korea, forcing the Goryeo royal family to flee to Kanghwa Island near Seoul. After twenty-five years of struggle, the royal family finally surrendered. The following 150 years saw continued Goryeo rule, but under the control of the Mongols. Korea's English name was derived during the Goryeo period (A.D. 918–1392).

After the death of the last Mongolian Emperor Mongke in 1259, the Mongol Empire broke up into the Golden Horde of Batu Khan (Genghis Khan's grandson), inhabiting the Russian lands; the Kingdom of Ugedey (Genghis Khan's son), who had conquered East Turkestan and Uzbek lands, and the Yuan State of Kubla Khan, which included the Mongolian and Chinese territories. Once Kubla Khan had pacified China, he turned his sights on other countries of Asia and conquered the empires where Vietnam, Laos, Cambodia, and Indonesia are located today. He invaded Korea and used it as a base in an attempt to conquer Japan, but he failed. Unlike Genghis Khan's, his army consisted mostly of infantry, with little cavalry, and he was also the first Mongolian ruler to have a navy.

Perhaps he also had in his possession Subudai's two-wheeled vehicle of molybdenum and tungsten.

Technological Wonders of Ancient China

It appears that the Mongols brought the mysterious metal vehicle from China. Subudai shed enough blood and spent sufficient time in China to loot the country of its treasures. He followed the teaching of the Universal Ruler, who once said that "man's greatest good fortune is to chase and defeat his enemy, seize his total possessions, leave his married women weeping and wailing, ride his gelding, and use the bodies of his women." At the same time, we need to remember that the Mongols did not persecute people for being Muslim, Buddhist, or Christian. Their capital of Karakorum contained a Muslim mosque, a Buddhist temple, and quite possibly a Christian church. Theirs was a ruthless, merciless empire, yet it assimilated other cultures and tolerated other faiths, unlike some modern nations.

At one time in its history, China was the world's most technologically advanced society. Indeed, for much of ancient times and the Middle Ages, China was significantly more advanced than Europe. Many important innovations were developed in ancient China, including the mariner's compass, the clock, the wheelbarrow, the crossbow, the animal harness, the printing press, ink, playing cards, gunpowder, and paper money. By A.D. 1000, the Chinese had invented seismographs to measure earthquakes. They possessed blast furnaces capable of producing cast iron.

But could they mine tungsten and produce tungsten steel?

In metallurgy, China has long held a leading position. Ancient Chinese scientists possessed knowledge of protochemistry and alchemy. Medicine and chemistry in ancient China were closely related to alchemy. Ancient Chinese metallurgical chemistry and alchemy is a subject of international research.

China has deposits of all minerals known in the world. There are verified reserves of 151 different minerals. On September 18, 2000, the Chinese *People's Daily* newspaper informed the world that Chinese geologists had discovered world-class mineral deposits in a part of the ancient Silk Road, the Hexi Corridor, in northwestern China. The actual reserves of nickel, copper, cobalt, platinum, tungsten, and gold in the corridor could be twice as large as the verified discoveries.

Luoyang, one of the seven ancient cities in China, lies in the northwestern part of Henan province. Deposits of molybdenum, aluminum, and tungsten are abundant there. Jiangxi Province in southeast China also has rich mineral resources, including tungsten, selenium, tellurium, rubidium, and lithium.

The ancient Chinese developed methods for the manufacture of steel that have only recently been matched in the West, such as a method for converting cast iron into steel by blowing air on the molten metal, which re-

Mongols at war with Turks and Persians.

duces the carbon content.

The ancient Chinese developed other technologies that were fantastically advanced for the time. According to the Xinhua Agency (Beijing), Chinese surgeons were performing craniotomies, surgical openings of the skull (difficult even in modern times), as early as four thousand years ago. There may be some credence to legends that the ancient Chinese possessed a non-intrusive medical device made of special glass capable of seeing inside human bodies.

We have yet to find evidence of the ancient production of tungsten alloys. If we do, then the mystery of Subudai's impenetrable vehicle will be solved.

There is another interesting episode of Subudai's biography that involves a search for the treasures of Genghis Khan.

A Pearl of Central Asia

Kyrgyzstan is nestled between Uzbek deserts, the Kazakh steppe, Tajikistan, and the outback of Western China. The majestic Tian Shan and Pamir mountain ranges stretch across this country.

Lake Issyk-Kul, a turquoise, unspoiled water reservoir, is located at an altitude of 5,291 feet and occupies the central part of the valley surrounded by the snow-capped Kungey Ala-Tau and Teskey Ala-Too mountain ranges. This vast lake lies in northeastern Kyrgyzstan, near the borders with China and Kazakhstan. The lake greatly affects the climate of the area. It doesn't freeze in winter; its waters are surprisingly warm and exceptionally transparent.

Issyk-Kul is truly a pearl of Central Asia. It is the second largest highland lake in the world, after Lake Titicaca in Peru. The lake's length is 110 miles, its width about forty miles, and it has a maximum depth of 1,110 feet.

This lake conceals numerous mysteries. Associated with it are Neanderthal camps, ancient burial mounds, clusters of cave drawings, mysterious dolls made from stones, and the ruins of strange settlements, towns, and graves hidden beneath the warm waters. Some date back to the first millennium. There are more than one hundred thousand petroglyphs on the shore of Lake Issyk-Kul dating back to the Neolithic period. Different nomadic tribal cultures that dwelt in the area left artifacts of their vanished ways of life. Archaeologists of Central Asia are aware of more than a dozen ancient and medieval sunken settlements on the bottom of the lake. One example is the town of Chigu, capital of the once powerful state of the Usuns. Investigators have discovered ceramics, earthen pottery, and bronze and copper artifacts, coins, and items from the Mongol period. The latter had their own name for Lake Issyk-Kul; they called it Femur-u-nor.

The Great Silk Road and the Mongols

The Great Silk Road functioned as an extremely important trade route from

China to the Roman Empire in the second century B.C. The road was about 4,300 miles long. Before the discovery of the sea route to India, the Silk Road was the most important connection between the Orient and the West. The most valuable commodity imported from China was silk; hence, the entire transcontinental trade route was named the Silk Road. But many other commodities were also traded: gold, ivory, exotic animals, plants, iron, furs, ceramics, jade, bronze objects, lacquer, precious stones, and glass. Religion, too, was a precious commodity of the great Silk Road, for Buddhism came to China from India along the northern branch of the trade route. And nowadays, scattered throughout the mountains and valleys of Kyrgyzstan, are ruins of numerous Zoroastrian, Buddhist, and Nestorian Christian monuments. There are still ruins of three ancient towns on the great Silk Road: Navekat, Suyab, and Balasagun.

The geographic location of Kyrgyzstan assured its significance on the Great Silk Road. Thus, from the very beginning, three branches of the road ran through the area.

In the thirteenth century, Mongol warriors under Genghis Khan invaded and devastated Kyrgyzstan. They destroyed irrigation systems, laid waste to towns, and turned farms to dust. There were settlements and caravanserai on the shores of Issyk-Kul, along the Silk Road, from the seventh century B.C. The towns prospered, the trade thrived—and then came the vicious and merciless Mongol hordes. The devastation inflicted on the territory was so harsh that the populations and cultures of Central Asia did not begin to recover until the Russian expansion there in the nineteenth century.

But before their prosperous towns were annihilated, the rich inhabitants hid their treasures, either in the soil or on the bottom of the beautiful lake. Who knows what fate befell those who buried their treasures away from the greedy hands of the invaders?

The Templars on the Lake

The search for the treasures has never stopped since the Mongols arrived on the shores of the lake ages ago. What sort of treasures were the Mongols looking for? None other than Subudai Bagatur searched for the treasures in Issyk-Kul's waters. China was ordered to provide skilled divers for Subudai's project. He was looking for the alleged hidden riches of the Templars. The legends had it that the Nestorian Christians had reached the lake and founded a monastery on the northern shore.

The ancient cemeteries discovered in the area cover the period from the middle of the thirteenth to the middle of the fourteenth century. There is a macabre legacy associated with the community of the Nestorian Christians: the Black Death that killed nearly half of the European population is believed to have spread from the hot, arid plains of central Asia, and the first known victims of the plague were probably a community of Nestorian Christians at Issyk-Kul. But the plague did not enter the Silk Road at the time of the Subudai's sojourn at the lake; the first victims were recorded in 1338.

Apparently, the Nestorians were aiding the Templars in building a castle somewhere on an island in Issyk-Kul. Here, supposedly, was the place where the Templars brought their fabulous treasures. The Knights Templar were a tremendously influential and powerful religious monastic military order that was formed as a result of the Crusades. Their wealth, limitless powers, and influence caused them to have prominent enemies. They were destroyed by Philip IV of France and Pope Clement V, and by 1314, they were gone, but not forgotten, from the European scene.

We will not explore the countless myths and legends about the order, but it would be of great interest to historians to find out what the fearsome Mongol commander knew about the Templars. They did meet on the Polish battlefield of Liegnitz, but the knights were no match for the Mongol armies.

Perhaps one of the imprisoned knights knew too much about the treasures hidden by his order in the Issyk-Kul and revealed the information under torture.

Treasures of the Nestorians

Gifts being presented to Genghis Khan by Russian dukes.

Nestorian Christianity flourished in China for several hundred years. The sect's followers spread out from Syria and founded colonies in the cities along the Silk Road through Central Asia. When Emperor Constantine made Christianity the official religion of the Roman Empire in the middle of the fourth century, he suppressed Hellenistic teachings and alchemy, among other things, as being pagan. The Nestorians, a sect of dissident Christians, smuggled out forbidden manuscripts to Persia in A.D. 400.

In 1218, Genghis Khan sent his "hound" Jebe and a large military detachment to the Chu Valley. Ugedey, one of the sons of the Ruler of the Universe, was a participant in the military operation. Their goal was to take the town of Balasagun. This town appeared in the ninth to eleventh centuries and became the capital of the Karakhanid Kaganat (empire) of Central Asia. Local Christians, together with monks of the Suyab Abbey near Balasagun, knew quite well the enemy that was coming their way and fled, taking their treasures with them. They organized a convoy of two hundred camels loaded with gold and jewels, and traveled, rather quickly, along the north shore of Lake Issyk-Kul toward Kashgar. This place is 4,200 feet above sea level in a cul-de-sac formed by the Tian Shan, Pamir, and Kunlun ranges. It was a major Silk Road town and a crossroads for invading armies.

Fishermen on Issyk-Kul lake in Kyrgyzstan.

The Christians never reached it, because another Mongol detail was approaching from the Santash mountain pass, over the watershed between the Ili and Issyk-Kul basins. The trapped Christians decided to hide their treasure. Part of it was buried in an Armenian Christian Abbey in the area. Another part of the treasure was hidden in the coastal waters. The remaining treasure was taken to a cave in the mountains. There was a river that ran into this cave, and the Christians were able to divert its waters for a while. They hid the treasure in the cave, probably underground; then they placed stone slabs over the hiding place. They marked one slab with a cross and then covered everything with soil. The river was again allowed to run into the cave, and the treasure was saved or lost, depending on one's point of view.

Treasures of the Universal Ruler

In 1227, Genghis Khan was severely injured and died shortly after falling from a horse. It has been largely accepted by historians that he died while fighting in Xixia, a territory bordering on current Ningxia and Inner Mongolia (both autonomous Chinese regions). Some legends have it that he was buried on the Ordos Plateau (Inner Mongolia) of China and that a shrine was built there. There are conflicting accounts of why the Universal Ruler chose the area. Some state that because of its beauty, he chose it as the place to be buried. There were to be no tombs for Mongol noblemen after their death, but imperial temples were built in order to permit commemoration of royal ancestors.

The exact gravesite of Temudjin is one of archaeology's lasting mysteries. To conceal the actual gravesite, eight hundred soldiers, who in turn were killed to ensure that Genghis Khan's rest was undisturbed, supposedly massacred every one of the two thousand people who attended his funeral. Virgins (their precise quantity undetermined) were entombed with the Mongol leader. The Mongols rode horses back and forth over his grave to forever hide it, and the treasures buried with Temudjin. As a rule, when any Mongolian nobleman died, his burial immediately became a taboo subject, but not to the extent of Temudjin's.

There have been reports recently that American scientists have found a possible Temudjin gravesite in Mongolia, but could not proceed with their investigations because of problems with Mongolian authorities. Some Mongol researchers also point to the Altai Mountains as the burial place of Genghis Khan. Some of his belongings were buried in Ordos as a diversion.

Universal Recognition

China has had a special relationship with the legacy of the Universal Ruler. Most rulers of China, including the Ming and Qing Dynasties, the Kuomintang Republican regime, and the Communists, gave official recognition and support to the founder of the Mongol Empire—even after the collapse of the Mongol-established Yuan Dynasty of China. The Red Guards of the Cultural Revolution had no such respect and did destroy some important artifacts from Genghis Khan's times.

Even today, one can learn much from the visit to Dongsheng, China, and Genghis Khan's mausoleum. The Chinese have researched the legacy of the Mongol empire, and it behooves researchers in the West to learn what the Chinese scientists have discovered.

For example, there are experts in China who discount Mongolia as a burial place of the Ruler of the Universe. One skeptic is Luo Xinyou, a professor at the Institute of Minorities at China's Academy of Social Sciences in Beijing. According to him, a Mongolian legend suggests that Genghis Khan was buried secretly in a mountainous region (*Agence France Press*, August 23, 2001). But what mountainous region?

Scientists in Kyrgystan believe that the treasures and the body of the Universal Ruler were actually hidden at the bottom of Lake Issyk-Kul.

Hiding the Treasure

There are old Kyrgyz legends about how Ugedey, one of the sons of Genghis Khan, prepared a coffin made of a very hard and durable material. His father's body, along with treasures of gold and jewels, was put into the coffin and buried on the bottom of the lake. But there were more Mongol treasures to hide, and that is precisely what the son did. He placed the jewels and gems in a mountain cave that was later flooded.

There are reports that the KGB and the Geological Council of the Kyrgyz SSR were engaged in the search for Genghis Khan's treasures. *Pravda*, the well-known Soviet newspaper, ran an article on August 24, 1975. Titled "Return to the Secret," it informed the Soviets that the Ministry of Internal Affairs was searching for Genghis Khan's treasures in Lake Issyk-Kul.

Interesting details of the Soviet treasure hunt in the area in the early 1950s are reported on an obscure but very informative Kyrgyz ecological website, and it contains the information about this search for the treasures of the Universal Ruler. It was conducted by the Geological Department of the Kyrgyzstan Soviet Republic, based on a map the Red Chinese gave to their Soviet allies.

Tyup village was supposedly the location of the hidden treasure. Allegedly, the gold and silver were hidden under Kaznak, a huge rock. However, it is unclear whether the treasure the Soviets were trying to find was

Genghis Khan.

that of the Nestorians (most likely, because the people who hid it were described as being chased by nomads) or the Mongols.

Soviet Hunt Is Ended

The map was very poor and nothing was discovered, probably because the local inhabitants secretly and skillfully sabotaged the work. The area was surrounded by barbed wire, and guards were placed to protect the treasures. The biggest obstacle, however, was Stalin's death in 1953 and the turmoil that followed. In 1973, a popular Soviet newspaper, *Trud*, published an article about treasures hidden throughout the Soviet Union. Tyup was mentioned as the location where Genghis Khan's treasure was buried. The information was based on Soviet secret police files from the 1930s.

Some hushed-up activities, conducted by Kyrgyz geologists, took place in 1976 and 1977. The geologists researched ancient legends and looked for the treasure in the area of Kurmentu Canyon. There were once gold and silver mines, but the geologists were looking for treasures, and apparently, found some proof, but they needed input from archaeologists.

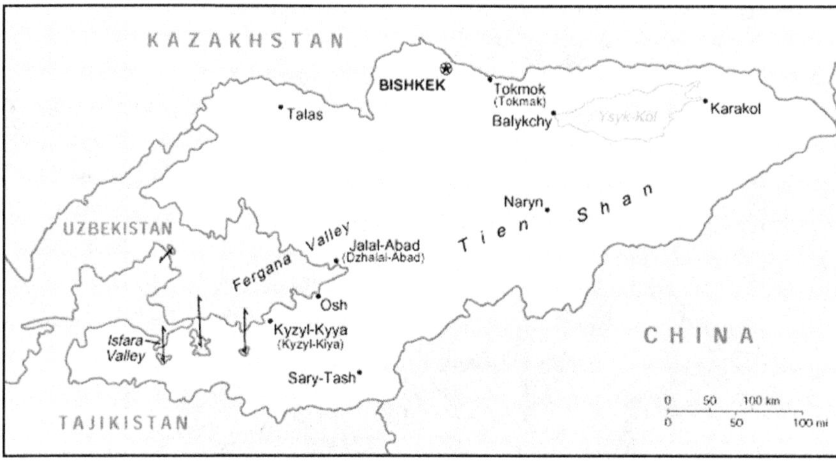

Map of Kyrgyzstan.

There have been free-lancers as well, especially after the fall of the USSR, because the new Civic Code of the Kyrgyz Republic states that anyone who finds the treasure has the right to fifty percent of the treasure's value.

Do Not Disturb

Whatever one's opinion of the Mongol conquests may be, I think we can all agree that looting or disturbing sacred ancient graves is not the answer to finding out the truth about the past. Modern Mongolians will not look kindly at anyone who would disturb the burial ground of their ancient leader.

This is their tradition—no one is allowed to lay hands on the bones of their ancestors—and their obedience to the will of Genghis Khan. He did not want any sign of his grave to be left after his death lest his everlasting peace be disturbed. There is a Mongol legend that the Universal Ruler will be reborn after eight hundred years from the day of his death.

Actually, that's not too long from now.

Chapter 5

The Lost Gold of Russia's Last Emperor

ALEXANDER VASILYEVICH KOLCHAK was a brave and bright young officer of the Russian Imperial Navy who took part in dangerous Arctic explorations, defended Russia's Port Arthur against the Japanese, and as the vice-admiral in command of the Russian Black Sea Fleet, valiantly set minefields next to the Turkish shores in World War I. Then came the February revolution of 1917, and later the same year the Bolsheviks grabbed power away from the weak but democratic provisional government. A very bloody civil war broke out in the former Russian Empire. Fortunes and treasures were lost or hidden in the most unlikely places, to save them from the various armies, warlords, bandits, and adventurers.

The trail of the imperial gold in the admiral's possession begins in November 1918 when Kolchak proclaimed himself the Supreme Ruler of Russia and commander-in-chief, establishing an autocratic military dictatorship. He also promoted himself to the rank of admiral. Kolchak's adversaries and bitter enemies were the Bolsheviks and the Red Army.

Kolchak's government controlled the area from Lake Baikal to the River Volga (Kolchakia, as Vladimir Lenin referred to it) and had the support of the Czechoslovak Legion, which controlled the Trans-Siberian railroad.

In April 1919, the Red Army began a counteroffensive against Kolchak's troops and forced them to flee the Urals. Kolchak retreated east, attempting to escape Russia through Vladivostok.

The Czar's imperial treasure was transported in 28 or 29 railroad cars under the guard of Kolchak's armored train. The treasure consisted of 505 tons of the Russian Imperial Bank's gold bullion and gold powder, as well as some jewels of the czars. Kolchak paid for military supplies and provisions straight from this Russian Imperial reserve, which was seized by the White Guard forces in the city of Kazan in August 1918.

Kolchak retreated to Irkutsk, losing most of his troops along the way. In December 1919, Kolchak was stopped at the town of Nizhneudinsk. Local Red partisans assumed control of the town, eager to grab Kolchak and "his" gold bullion. They declared the town an independent republic, but the Czechoslovak legionnaires whisked Kolchak and the gold out of there.

The train reached Irkutsk (to the west of Lake Baikal), accompanied by a small detachment of legionnaires.

On January 15, 1920, French General Janin and the Czech General Jan Syrovy handed Kolchak over to the Irkutsk Provisional Government, friendly to the Soviets, whose revolutionary military committee executed the admiral and his prime minister and took possession of all of Siberia. Admiral Kolchak faced his executioners with composure and courage. He was shot on February 7, 1920.

On the Trail of the Imperial Gold

Who acquired possession of "Kolchak's gold"? The Czechoslovaks, who were evacuated from Russia soon thereafter, allegedly got some of it. The French General Maurice Janin, Commander-in-Chief of the Allied troops in Siberia, received one-third of the gold bullion from the Russian Imperial treasury. This gold was rumored to have become the first national treasury of the newly created country of Czechoslovakia. The Czechoslovak legionnaires

supposedly turned the rest of the gold in to the socialist revolutionaries and the Mensheviks of Irkutsk, allies of the Soviets (at the time), and the Mensheviks handed the gold to the arriving Soviets. But I have found no conclusive evidence that that is what happened.

The Japanese Connection

There are at least two conflicting conjectures as to the whereabouts of the imperial gold.

Leonid Petrov, a Russian researcher of Asia at the Australian State University, believes some 182 tons of Russian gold (worth 191 million golden rubles) settled in Japanese banks. In order to destroy any proof of such transactions, Japanese Finance Minister Takahashi promptly ordered the Imperial Mint in Osaka to melt this gold into Japanese nuggets and coins.

The Japanese never cared for Kolchak, for they did not want to see any viable Russian government in Asia. Yet they received hundreds of tons of Russian gold from him, in payment for weapons (which, apparently, never were sent).

On the Bottom of the Beloved Sea

There is another theory as to what happened to at least some of Kolchak's gold.

Before proceeding to Irkutsk, Kolchak's forces reached Lake Baikal. The magnificent lake is almost four hundred miles long and holds one-fifth of the world's lake waters. Lake Baikal is the world's oldest, deepest, largest, and most unique lake. It is situated nearly in the center of Asia in a huge stone bowl set 445 meters above sea level.

Yuri Metelin, a Russian journalist, published an article about Kolchak's sojourn there in *NLO* magazine in 1999.

Kolchak's troops were exhausted and in ill health. They wanted to reach Manchuria, where they would feel safe. All they needed to do was to cross the area close to the southern shores of the lake. But the territory was under the control of the Red Army. The retreating White Army troops had only one path to safety: they had to cross the frozen lake on foot.

The gold and jewels were unloaded from the train and distributed among those officers and soldiers loyal to Kolchak.

They did not get far before terrible cold winds started to blow across the icy fields and hummocks of Baikal. The southern part of the lake is only thirty kilometers wide, but the freezing winds buried most of Kolchak's troops.

In the spring, when the ice melted, the dead White Guard troops were submerged, and the gold bullion went down with them. Bodies of those who drown in the lake are rarely found: microorganisms in Baikal devour dead flesh within hours.

The survivors, including two officers named Bogdanov and Drankovich, hid the gold they managed to save in the cellar of a church located near the lakeshore. Then they led the rest of the soldiers to a nearby sandpit and shot them to death, execution style. Soon thereafter the officers quarreled and a bloody fight ensued. Bogdanov killed Drankovich and later fled to the United States.

Back in the USSR

In 1959, Bogdanov arrived in the Soviet Union under an alias, and with the assistance of an American engineer was able to retrieve some of the treasure hidden in the church. They loaded a Jeep with one hundred kilograms of Kolchak's gold and left. Apparently, Bogdanov and Smith tried to cross the border into Turkey, but the Soviet border troops killed the Russian. Smith made it out of the USSR but left the gold and his vehicle behind.

Deep underwater exploration of Lake Baikal in the 1970s revealed a bottle full of gold powder at a depth of one thousand meters. A gold bar was also detected. However, it is unlikely anything will be retrieved from the bottom of the deep-water lake.

Another Train, Another Mystery

Then there is the mystery of the missing gold reserve of the Saint Petersburg Mint. In the fall of 1916 it was sent to Moscow, on the orders of the Czar, who feared a German invasion of his capital. Valery Verkhorubov of *NLO* magazine (1999) has assembled the best version of this episode I have found so far.

The train carrying this gold reserve left Saint Petersburg just before the February 1917 revolution. According to the cargo bills of the Saint Petersburg Mint, there were 1,360 kilograms of gold bars and 67 kilograms of gold coins aboard.

Finding Moscow in a state of anarchy, the officer in charge of the precious cargo received orders from the czar to take the train to the city of Ekaterinburg in the Ural Mountains. There the gold was to be transferred to the Russian Imperial Bank. The officer of the Russian counterintelligence service followed the orders. But the gold disappeared without a trace...

Nicholas II was forced to sign a document of abdication after being brought down by political unrest. In April 1918, the Bolshevik government decided to move the Imperial family to Ekaterinburg. In July 1918, local Bolsheviks in Ekaterinburg executed the entire royal family under orders of Lenin. The bodies were hidden for many years and have only recently been found and identified.

The Bolsheviks followed the trail of the brave officer and the train with the gold reserve. They kidnapped him from China, after learning his name in 1919, when the Ekaterinburg Cheka (Soviet secret police, forerunner of the KGB) conducted detailed investigations. Apparently the young man did not betray his secrets, and the Bolsheviks were not able to find out where he and his soldiers hid the gold.

The officer (whose name was not recorded) decided to hide the gold in the Urals. The train was taken to a branch-line of the railroad, where the guards unloaded the treasure at a remote crossing. They buried the gold in the ground, and the officers left Russia with a few gold bars.

The search for the czar's gold has never stopped ever since the secret police learned of its fate, but so far it has not been found. The missing gold reserve of the Saint Petersburg Mint is still hidden somewhere in the ground, not far from Ekaterinburg.

Part Two
Mysteries of the Eurasian Inner Earth

Chapter 6

Mysteries of the Jihlava Catacombs

Jihlava is a town in the Czech Republic. It is the center of the Vysocina Region, located on the Jihlava River on the ancient frontier between Moravia and Bohemia. The castles, chateaus, and manors of Moravia have a glorious past and pride themselves on their unique architecture. But the town has a unique historical monument that has placed it on the paranormal map of the world.

Ancient Catacombs

Jihlava is the oldest mining town in the Czech Republic, where, according to legends, the silver mines were worked as early as A.D. 799. Jihlava was located on important trade routes, and after the silver mines closed, it became a center of regional business.

Jihlava's underground passages (*Jihlavské podzemí*, in Czech) are a significant part of the town's ancient architecture. These catacombs, second in length in the Czech Republic, are located directly below the old section of the town. Their total length is twenty-five kilometers, covering an area of fifty thousand square meters. The catacombs, believed by some to be created by the joining of the cellars, are fascinating examples of the Gothic building style—unless some of the hidden tunnels were built in the mists of time.

The catacombs have several floors. The first floor is two to four meters underground, the second floor is four to six meters underground, and below some parts of the second floor is even a third floor, with a depth of eight to fourteen meters underground.

Why the catacombs were built is still a mystery. Some historians thought for a long time that the catacombs used to be a part of the silver mines, while others believed that the corridors were built for military purposes.

The multiple-level catacombs are cut into hard rock. The first-level corridors were built during the fourteenth century, the second and third-level corridors were added in the sixteenth century, and, finally, during the seventeenth century, some of the corridors were reinforced with brick foundations.

In the middle of each corridor, there is a shallow gutter to drain the water collected from the walls or trickled down from the surface. Shafts going up to the surface provide air ventilation for the corridors. Many of the corridors have access to underground water wells. The temperature in the catacombs ranges between eight and twelve degrees Celsius.

But in addition to the main, man-height corridors, there is a network of smaller tunnels, forming the town's sewage system. As the centuries passed, the catacombs were abandoned or converted into sewage tunnels; some corridors were filled with debris and trash. Floods ensued as the drainage system was damaged.

In the 1960s almost all of the corridors were reinforced with concrete, all of the debris was removed, and the medieval drain system restored.

The catacombs were finally opened to the public in 1991.

The Shining

In 1978, a group of amateur speleologists discovered the so-called "shining corridor." The walls of the corridor are covered with a milky coating which emits a greenish glow after exposure to light. The vaulted corridor lies about 11 meters under the street level; it is 2.1 meters wide and 2.9 meters high.

For quite a long time, no one could figure out the reason for the shining corridor's fluorescence; stories and rumors circulated, trying to explain it. According to one of them, the fluorescence is due to phosphorus released from the bones of the monks buried in one of the corridors above; according to another story, an unknown organic substance causes the radiation.

Then, experts of the Mineralogy Department of the Faculty of Natural Sciences from Charles University (Prague) arrived to help solve the mystery. Their analysis of collected samples revealed that it is a man-made substance with a long afterglow interval. The substance, containing zinc sulfite and barium, had been used in the mortar mixture applied onto the walls.

Just what purpose the coating may have had and who authored the idea cannot be ascertained. The experts assumed that it was to serve as an emergency orientation lighting at the time when the catacombs were used as an air-raid shelter, or that some kind of illumination tests were performed there.

Some Czech speleologists believe that the luminescence is caused by fungi or microbial activity.

Eerie Music and a Baffling Stairwell

But the Prague experts' explanation cannot account for the organ music that is heard at midnight in one of the corridors. According to Russian journalist Igor Shamshin of the ITAR-TASS, who in 1997 investigated the strange phenomena heard and seen in the catacombs, the underground monument contains mysteries and ancient legends that modern science has not been able to solve.

Czech archaeologists heard organ music in a tunnel located at the depth of ten meters. There are no rooms nearby where an organ could be hidden;

the archaeologists searched the area thoroughly. Later the scientists were checked by psychologists who found no sign of any acoustic hallucinations.

Then there is the issue of the "shining stairwell," discovered in one of the least explored passages. The existence of this passage was completely unknown even to those who live in the area and know the tunnels well. The stairwell was manufactured in early medieval times, and it emits bright fluorescence in the darkness. No phosphorus was found in the probes the scientists took from the material.

One of the archaeologists, an old acquaintance of Shamshin, surreptitiously led him to the passage. They left Shamshin's automobile near the castle in old Jihlava and approached a small house situated on a rock. They passed a small room full of archaeological tools and equipment, and approached an ancient door, coated with iron. Shamshin's companion asked him to be extremely careful as they entered the catacombs. They used a powerful flashlight, illuminating narrow underground galleries. Water drops were falling from the ceilings.

The men walked for half an hour. Often they encountered obstructions consisting of rocks and broken bricks. The archaeologist advised Shamshin to keep track by looking at the numbers painted on the walls and reflected in the light. Then abruptly, the flashlight was turned off. The scientist asked Shamshin to follow him and be prepared to see a miracle. Taking the journalist by hand, he led him through complete darkness. They made some 20 steps, passed around a partition, and the archaeologist turned the flashlight on again.

In front of them was a dilapidated narrow stone stairwell. It did not look to Shamshin as anything out of the ordinary in the beginning, but then he saw that the stairwell was emitting an ever-increasing reddish-orange glow. The flashlight was turned off again, but the shining glow did not subside. They spent some time next to the mysterious stairwell, to be certain that the shining did not cease. It did not; the intensity of it remained the same. Their feet wet, feeling quite cold, the archaeologist and Shamshin returned to the small house.

There is a mention of "something like a ghost that had appeared in front of luminescent wall" in a Czech report (P. Demčák (17 10. 1996): *Zpráva o paranormálním jevu,* 2 str. Archív ČSS). The writer explored the catacombs in the fall of 1996.

Is the stairwell made of the same material as the substance, containing zinc sulfite and barium, used in the mortar applied onto the walls? Who is playing the eerie music? Do the tunnels lead to other rooms at greater depths? We have no answers as yet.

Chapter 7

Russia's *Diggeri*

There are countless secrets that lay hidden under the former Soviet Union.

"Digger," in English, means one who digs. There are people in Russia who have borrowed the word, changed it slightly, and call themselves *diggeri*. Theirs is a cryptic world; they have their own traditions, philosophy, and experiences. The diggeri explore Russia's subterranean world. They quite frequently find incredible things. Their explorations of the gigantic subterranean structures of Moscow have been exposed and written about since the fall of the Soviet Union, but the diggeri are found all over Russia, as well as the former Soviet republics. Most of their reports are hidden from curious journalists.

Giant Rats

Some consider their tales to be legends. But the reports of gigantic rats that populate underground Moscow have been confirmed more than once. Vadim

Mikhailov, one of the founders of the Muscovite diggeri, and his comrades encountered the beasts in the tunnels under the city's zoo.

There were five gigantic rats, and the diggeri saved their lives by tossing metal rods at the monsters and fleeing the scene. The explorers had been descending into the subterranean world for 19 years prior to that and had never encountered anything similar. The mutants, as Mikhailov described the rats, were about 65 centimeters long, not counting the tail. One was probably a female, for its proportions were smaller, and the color lighter.

The diggeri immediately alerted the city government, notified television media, and reported the location to the police. The authorities closed the tunnels only four days later. The rats were observed in the tunnels leading to the zoo, the American Embassy, and the Russian "White House" (Parliament).

Several days later the diggeri, in their headquarters, received anonymous phone calls from people who claimed to be former Soviet military officers. They provided detailed descriptions of the entrances and passageways of the military underground bunkers that formed the defensive complex under Moscow and its vicinity. The abandoned structures were located next to spent nuclear fuel storage casks. This is where many uncanny events have taken place. If the former officers are to be believed, they had seen thousands of gigantic rats below Moscow. Their description of the mutant rats was almost identical to what Mikhailov and his diggeri observed under the zoo. The explorers were eager to undertake an expedition to the storage casks, but would do so only when they obtained weapons.

Other Entities

Mikhailov described the subterranean life forms he and his colleagues have encountered through the years. There are "bags," "crawlers," something dubbed *glyuki*, and other ghostly, phantom-like formations. There are small "stars" that appear suddenly from the surrounding darkness and extend their tentacles toward people, as if trying to emit energy. The term used by diggeri is "underground adrenaline."

Sometimes, at great depths under the city, diggeri see illumination from flashlights at the other end of a tunnel. But who else would dare descend so far under the surface? When diggeri approach the "flashlights," they go out, leaving nothing but silence.

In the old, abandoned tunnels, diggeri found strange, mysterious signs on the walls. Who drew them, when, and why?

As they wandered in the tunnels under an old cemetery, the diggeri observed ephemeral, ghost-like creatures that extended their arms toward the explorers, and then "fell into" the floor, or water.

Mikhailov mentioned the so-called *khokhriki*, tiny creatures that appear on the photographs after the films used underground are developed. He does not believe that this is an optical illusion.

The diggeri are not indifferent to the mystical world. Once they decided to confirm the legend of the White Nun.

There was a monastery called Nikolo-Vishsky near the Russian city of Ryazan. The Communists closed it and built a Young Pioneers summer camp at the site. According to local legend, the abbess cursed the camp, and along with a few other nuns physically walled themselves off behind the walls of the abbess's house, in the 1920s. Strange phenomena have been observed in the area of the camp ever since. Before storms, the sound of a bell comes from underground, and singing by the walled-off women has been reported.

After that the ghost of the White Nun appears. It is two to three meters tall and walks from the site of the old church to the abbess's house. The sighting is not frequent; the White Nun is sighted only at night, but many people have seen her.

When Mikhailov's diggeri arrived at the site, and during their stay, they saw the ghost three times. Usually they do not investigate mystical reports and legends, but in this case they decided to proceed. They discovered an underground passageway that led to the abbess's house, which was underground by then. The passageway was located under the alley where the White Nun was sighted. But getting inside the burial area was not that simple: flashlights went out, the video camera stopped working, and bricks from inside the burial site flew out straight at the diggeri. The first of the group who entered the site fainted for several minutes and had to be dragged out by his colleagues.

Mikhailov's people call themselves Diggers of the Underground Planet. It is worth mentioning here that they also discovered Ivan the Terrible's lost torture chamber, catacombs and passageways; a pond that was allegedly the site of a mass suicide; and a strange site under Sukharevskaya Square in Moscow.

There are so many more abandoned industrial locations around Moscow for them to explore, so many secret tunnels and mysterious offshoots of the enigmatic Moscow subway system to map, that I am certain we are going to hear more from Mikhailov and his diggeri.

Latvian Discoveries

Diggeri in the Latvian city of Riga recently discovered a gruesome medieval prison under the city. It was located underneath Kalkyu Street, and according to legends, it was where the plague originated to engulf the city in the fourteenth century. The journalists who accompanied local diggeri to the underground dungeons reported strange feelings of being watched by thousands of unseen eyes. This is where thieves, adulteresses, and murderers were tortured before their execution. There are numerous passageways that lead to unexplored areas of the old city.

German historian and SS member Otto Rahn, who studied the history of the Knights Templar on Hitler's orders, believed that the knights had concealed their treasures somewhere in Latvia.

According to Rahn, the subterranean vaults of Riga (as well as certain Latvian castles) were built according to the sacred geometry of the Knights Templar. Local diggeri are aware of the hypothesis. Some Latvian journalists are of the opinion that the German scientist was on to something interesting.

Rahn, a protégé of Himmler, died a mysterious death at the age of thirty-five in the Tyrolean Mountains. An enigmatic person, he was known for his study of the Cathars, the Montsegur, and their secrets.

Sometimes the Latvian diggeri find forgotten Soviet missile silos, such as the one in the remote province of Eleya, ten kilometers from the border. The most valuable equipment had been taken away by teams of "black pathfinders" years before. Konstantin Buglov, perhaps the most famous of the Latvian diggers, has also explored the sinister Zvardskaya Zone, where the Soviets tested their secret weapons for 50 long years.

Diggeri of Russia's Battle Sites

They are also known as "black pathfinders" and "trophy people." Digging through the vast lands of the former USSR, they frequently find mass graves dating back to World War II. They disturb the peace of the deceased, and some of them (not many are willing to talk about such matters) recall unusual, terrifying visions. This variety of subterranean exploration began in the late 1980s. Excavations of the military cemeteries were illegal, but the country was falling apart and enforcement of the law was weak.

But even in such a distant period as 1970, there was a case of some hunters who met an elderly woman near the Sinyavskiye Heights, where fierce battles had taken place almost thirty years before. The woman told them that she had lived in the area before the war, and was now searching

for some village cemetery. As they exchanged good-byes, the woman read the hunters' fortune, and left. Some minutes later the hunters noticed that she left no footprints in the snow.

The trophy people report that when they conduct their excavations of the military cemeteries during spells of warm weather, rain pours down on them.

In 1985 something inexplicable occurred over the German military cemetery in the Mikhailovskoye settlement. The day before some black pathfinders had operated in the area. At night, a thin ray of light was suddenly emitted from a strange apparatus hovering in the sky. All of the village dogs started barking wildly, while power outages cut off the flow of electricity to the settlement. Some 15 minutes later the ray vanished and the mysterious apparatus departed. Half an hour later two military aircraft flew very low over Mikhailovskoye; no one had ever seen such planes there before.

One episode took place in the Novgorod region when a group of diggeri approached a German military cemetery behind a small village. The weather was freezing, although the snow had not yet fallen. Suddenly they observed a white silhouette of an indefinite shape, about three meters tall, rising from the corner of a house in the village. The distance between the pathfinders and the ghost was about seventy meters. The mysterious shape slowly and noiselessly moved to the opposite direction, away from the astonished diggeri. Every fifteen meters the ghost would stop and alter its contours. At first it looked like a gigantic cow, then a horse, and finally a man. Changing its shape in this manner, the ghost noiselessly crossed the field and vanished into the forest.

In the Pskov region the diggeri wanted to excavate another abandoned German cemetery. As night approached, they saw an unusual black animal pacing up and down the river bank. The animal was something of a cross between a wild boar and a bear. It disappeared when the diggeri surrounded a bush where it was hiding.

In 1988 some diggeri in Belarus approached a mass grave. During the war many locals were executed and buried in such places. In the twilight hours the diggeri saw a man walking toward them on an abandoned village road. He wore an expensive suit and had a shapeless black stain instead of a face. He stopped some 15 meters from the trophy people, who shouted greetings to him. Suddenly the stranger moved sideways and noiselessly vanished in the roadside vegetation. The pine trees that grew at the side of the road were less than thirty centimeters apart, and it would have been quite impossible for a human being to crawl through them silently.

In 1997 a team of diggeri was on its way near the ruins of the Makaryev monastery near Lyuban. The monastery was completely destroyed during the war; only the foundations were left in the middle of the marsh. This site was considered cursed by the diggeri. When six of them approached the ruins in the twilight hours, they noticed a campfire up ahead. It was floating in the air. They had a very restless night; from 3:00 to 5:00 a.m. they heard bloodcurdling human screams in the forest. The impression they had was of someone being torn apart alive. One of the diggeri, who left for a few minutes to relieve himself, came back after three hours. He was scared, terrified of what he saw in the forest, but never told anyone what had actually happened to him.

Among Latvian diggeri who officially search for the weapons of World War II (for museums, for instance) there is a belief that one who finds and does not properly rebury the remains of fallen soldiers has bad luck. Such official diggeri in Russia, Latvia, and elsewhere very much dislike the trophy people, who are better equipped and behave like barbarians. The black pathfinders, for the most part, throw away the remains of fallen soldiers they encounter during their illegal excavations. It is weapons that interest the trophy people; they find eager buyers for the well-preserved arms and equipment abroad, including even unearthed tanks.

There are many groups in Russia and neighboring countries who look for the forgotten cemeteries of World War II so that they can preserve their memory, rebury the soldiers, and find the names of those who perished in the bloodiest war of the twentieth century. Sometimes their paths cross those who desecrate the memory and resting places of the fallen soldiers for monetary gain.

Raiders of Russia's Attics

This is another category of the diggeri. They explore the countless attics of Russia's aging buildings. The professionals research reference books and archives before they target a specific building. Their findings are often quite valuable: abandoned treasures, weapons, medals, coins, and so on. Revolutions, wars, invasions, and *coups d'etat* rocked Russia in the bloody twentieth century. People would look for places to hide their valuables; soldiers who came home from the front would take care to conceal their trophies. The attics above their apartments very often served the purpose. Later some of those who hid their treasures and belongings were arrested, sent to yet another war, or simply became forgetful in old age. Yet the valuables remained hidden in the attics; that is, until the diggeri came up the stairs.

In the major cities of Russia the attics have been cleaned out long ago, hence the diggeri embark to explore smaller cities and towns. There they still find jewelry from bygone times, coins, imperial swords, and much more. But they also find concealed corpses, drug paraphernalia, and victims of suicide and diseases. To dig through the age-old trash is seldom healthy, and diggeri find tuberculosis as often as ancient coins. They also report eerie encounters, but are very reluctant to go into details. Their lore is also full of stories about attic diggeri who found sizable treasures. This is what drives them to go on.

Chapter 8

Secrets of the Regenwurmlager

A few of the unsolved mysteries of World War II literally lie under our feet. Some below-ground structures, bunkers, and fortifications built by Nazi Germany contain secrets that have not been revealed until now, at least to the public. One such underground system of fortifications, built by the Germans, was discovered in Poland after the Nazis were crushed by Soviet troops in the area. Although fifty-seven years have passed since the discovery, we still know very little about the site.

The Regenwurmlager

Lubuskie Province (Wojewodztwo, or Voivodship, the term for an administrative province) is located in western Poland. The province borders the German state of Brandenburg. For centuries, this part of Poland was under Prussian control and formed a part of the province of Posen (Poznan, in Polish). After Poland was liberated following the defeat of Nazi troops by the Soviet Army, the area was returned. Germans who lived in the province

were forced out, and Poles from those eastern parts of Poland that were transferred to the Ukraine were later resettled in the Lubuskie province.

The main rivers of the region are the Odra (Oder, in German), running along the Polish-German corridor, and its tributaries, the Bobr and the Warta. The voivodship is the most forested area of Poland; its deep forests are full of lakes.

Miedzyrzecz is a small town on the Obra, a tributary of the Warta. The town dates back to the tenth century. To the west of Miedzyrzecz, in the Lubuskie Lake District (approximately 100 kilometers west of Poznan and 220 kilometers east of Berlin), stretches the powerful and enormous Odra/Warta line of Nazi underground fortifications, part of the Ostwall (East Wall) built to strengthen the Eastern Front and defend the Third Reich. This area is called the Miedzyrzecki Fortified Region (Miedzyrzecki Rejon Umocniony, in Polish). The Germans called it the Regenwurmlager (Earthworm Lair), code-named RL.

A very elaborate system of bunkers was built there in the 1930s and during the war. They are sometimes compared to the famous Maginot Line. There are reinforced underground corridors some fifty or more kilometers long, located thirty to fifty meters below ground. It is possible to visit part of the corridors near the village of Kalawa (Pniewo) about twelve kilometers southwest of Miedzyrzecz. Today, it is possible to see the "Scharnhorst" Bunkers, but only with an experienced and trained guide (there are multilingual guides at the site). There are exhibitions of military equipment from World War II—and bats.

There is actually a bat reserve ("Nietoperek") in the underground bunkers. More than thirty thousand bats of twelve different species make the reserve one of the largest winter camps of bats in Europe. The Communist Polish Government wanted to designate the underground passages as a dumping site for nuclear waste, but changed their plan after Polish scientists alerted their Western colleagues.

Few people realize that the tunnels are largely unexplored and contain traps designed long ago to kill those who wandered into the secret Nazi fortifications. Careless tourists have lost their lives when they fell prey to elaborate traps built by Nazi engineers.

The Miedzyrzecki Fortified Region (or MFR) consists of reinforced concrete lumps of bunkers, enormous steel domes, and kilometers of concrete poles. These are anti-tank barriers called zebow smoka (dragon teeth). About twenty-one of the bunkers were joined by a subway system at a depth of thirty to fifty meters. There is a labyrinth below the MFR that has been left largely undisturbed, save for the bats. The main tunnel (Main Traffic Road) extends down along the north-south line. It is basically an axis of tunnels. There are side tunnels that branch from the main tunnel and connect with the so-called "structure." Concrete stairs lead from the side tunnels to the surface part of the structure—Panzerwerk, a bunker.

The bunkers on the surface were equipped with war domes (their steel walls are twenty-five centimeters thick). The bunkers contained machine guns, flamethrowers, and grenade launchers. There were stockrooms, barracks, ambulances, a ventilation system, and an engine room. The underground portion of the MRF contained a lighting system, ventilation, sewage system, and communications. The structures were connected through the use of an electric train.

The multistoried concrete corridors may still hide secrets of German nuclear weapons research and development efforts at the close of WW II. The Red Army liberated this area from the Nazis in January 1945, and it remained in Soviet hands until 1993. According to them, there are still mysteries pertaining to the Miedzyrzecki Fortified Region.

There was a Jewish presence in Miedzyrzecz, too. A cemetery was established there in the mid-seventeenth century. It was vandalized during WW II, and there are no grave stones or structures there now. One matseva (sepulchral stone) was removed and placed in the Miedzyrzecz Museum. Others were in the forest near the cemetery.

There was a ghetto in the area during the war. Some Jews of Miedzyrzecz were transported to the Baranovichi Ghetto in the Novogrudok district of Byelorussia and were murdered there. On September 26, 1942, remaining Jews from the Biala Podlaska town ghetto in the Polish Lublin Province were deported to the ghetto in Miedzyrzecz and from there to the Treblinka death camp in November of 1942.

Of course, much has changed on the surface, especially after the fall of Communism, when Poland became a free nation. Where once one could find scars of the Nazi occupation and the presence of Soviet troops, today there are tourist hotels and museums. Instead of ammunition and mines, people find mushrooms and berries.

However, we are concerned with the mysteries that have remained locked in the underground structures built by the Third Reich. Unfortunately, we do not know what information about the Regenwurmlager is in the possession of the Urzad Ochrony Panstwa (UOP) (Office for State Protection), the Polish intelligence agency. We do not know if any findings have been shared with the Americans, NATO, or Germany's Intelligence Service (BND). An examination of the Soviet sources is in order, and here we may have more success.

A bunker entrance to the Regenwurmlager underground complex.

Info from Russian Sources

The territory was under the control of the Soviet armed forces stationed in Poland until 1993. Only the Soviet military administration was able to investigate the odd reinforced-concrete SS "city" discovered shortly after the end of the war. Yet the Soviets failed to undertake any systematic exploration of the Regenwurmlager. The Kremlin sent no instructions to do so, and the local commanders saw no need to volunteer their efforts.

But there was one Soviet military officer who wanted to uncover the secrets of the Nazi underground bunkers. Aleksandr Liskin descended into the tunnels of the Regenwurmlager; collected information, testimonies, and legends of the area; and shared his findings in an article published in the Russian newspaper *Sovershenno Sekretno* (no. 5, 1994). I researched other Russian publications, such as Nikolay Cherkashin's article in *Rossiyskaya Gazeta* (November 11, 1999), Aleks Bure's article in *Sekretniye Issledovaniya* (Byelorussia, April 2002), and Liskin's article in *Vokrug Sveta* magazine (no. 5, 1995). I also researched Soviet military publications and open sources.

Some current German sources were helpful for the names of towns and villages.

The Soviet troops stationed in Poland formed the so-called Northern Group of Forces (NGF). The NGF was established in June 1945. Until 1956, there were no legal regulations regarding the presence of Soviet troops in Polish territory. Soviet soldiers and the property utilized by them were beyond any control by the Polish authorities. Later agreements between the two countries regulated their legal status and movement.

Some NGF units were stationed in the tiny village of Keszyca (Kainscht, in German), near Miedzyrzecz. There was a Signal Brigade (five battalions) and a fuel depot; they used a territory of 119.4 hectares. The brigade was an elite Soviet military force that assisted the general staff in controlling Soviet troops in the huge European theater. There were a field radar station, barracks, warehouses, garages, and other buildings. The territory under the NGF control was transferred to the Polish government on May 12, 1993. Prior to 1945, it was a German military site, surrounded by forests.

Keszyca is a picturesque village surrounded by lakes and by forests full of berries and mushrooms. Under Nazi occupation, the village was also part of the Miedzyrzecki Fortified Region.

The German troops, according to local denizens, did not put up a stiff fight when the Red Army pushed into the area. The garrison of the Miedzyrzecki Fortified Region consisted of two regiments, security forces, and the school of the 3rd SS Panzer Division Totenkopf (Death's Head).

In October 1939, Hitler set up the SS field divisions that would later form the Waffen SS. Among them was the Totenkopfdivision. Its officers and soldiers perpetrated horrors that typify the Nazi terror in Europe. One battalion was stationed in the Nazi-occupied Soviet Union with the Kommandostab Reichsführer SS (Command Staff of the Reich Leader of the SS) and was charged with killing Jews. The Totenkopfdivision also took part in atrocities, mostly against partisans and enemy soldiers. Obviously, they expected no mercy from Soviet soldiers, and they were entitled to none.

A tunnel in the Regenwurmlager.

To escape being surrendered, the SS forces in the MFR began a hasty retreat. They disappeared in a matter of hours—but where to? The only road in the area had already been captured by tanks of the 44th Guard Tank Brigade of Gen. M. E. Katukov's First Guard Tank Army. The tank battalion of the brave Soviet commander, Maj. Alexey Karabanov, posthumously awarded the Hero of the Soviet Union medal, pierced the minefields surrounding the Regenwurmlager. He burned in his tank there in January 1945. Red Army soldiers under the command of Colonel Gusakovsky broke through this Nazi Maginot line, chasing Hitler's forces from the Polish land that had been under German domination for centuries.

But the Totenkopfdivision SS forces in the area disappeared without a trace…

Liskin's Investigation

Keszyca is located on a hill surrounded by a pine forest and Lake Keszyckie, and its beauty is breathtaking. In the early 1960s, when Col. Aleksandr Liskin visited the area, an air of mystery surrounded the lake.

An artillery regiment located in the vicinity, and a security official, Telyutko, who supervised the area for Miedzyrzecz authorities, represented the Polish military forces in the area. They transferred the territory to the Soviet forces for temporary use (which lasted until 1993). The Soviet commanders immediately undertook a scrupulous reconnaissance of the area. They made discoveries that amazed even the battle-hardened Soviet military.

First, near the lake, the Soviets found a reinforced concrete box that contained an isolated outlet for an underground power cable. The cable carried 380 volts at the time the Soviet engineers studied it. Then they found a concrete well that stored falling water. At the same time, reconnaissance discovered that the underground power communications came from Miedzyrzecz. But the engineers also believed that there might be a concealed autonomous electrical power station, its turbines moved by water falling into the well. There were rumors that the lake was somehow connected to the numerous nearby reservoirs, but the brigade lacked resources to confirm this.

Keszyca was then, as it is now, a quiet place, peaceful, and full of the aroma of the nearby forest. But rumors about the lake aroused Liskin's curiosity. He explored the area with the aid of local Soviet officers. After Liskin took a boat ride around the lake, he discovered even more mysteries.

From the eastern side of Lake Keszyckie, he saw powerful "hills" overgrown with young trees. They contained artillery caponnieres. The "hills"contained secret passageways leading to galleries below. Not far away, there were two tiny lakes—and nearby signs stating "Danger! Mines!"in two languages. According to Soviet field engineers, the "lakes" were actually entrances to the flooded underground city below. Then there was a very strange "island" in the middle of the lake. This island slowly drifted, as if held by anchor. The island was overgrown with pine trees and willows, and its area was no more than 50 meters. It seemed to Liskin that the island slowly and with difficulty rolled about in the black waters of the reservoir. The lake had an artificial addition that resembled an appendix. The water here was clearer, and measured two or three meters deep. It was still hard to see anything because fern-like weeds completely covered the bottom of the lake. There was a gray concrete tower in the middle of this little "bay"; it had served some purpose before, but now it contained only water.

Not for the Unwary

During the initial reconnaissance, Soviet military engineers discovered an entrance to the tunnels, disguised as a hill. They surmised that what lay before and under them was a complex structure, full of traps, including mines. Once a slightly inebriated Soviet sergeant major made a bet and rode his motorcycle through the mysterious tunnel. He was never heard from again. Liskin was more cautious, and he approached the brigade's commanders. He learned that the brigade's field engineers and communications technicians had not only descended into the tunnel, but had also walked it for dozens of kilometers. They discovered previously unknown entrances. Information about this expedition was kept secret. Liskin discussed the expedition with a staff officer, who told him that to preclude tragedies, the Soviets had installed a metal grating and armored panel on the opening to the tunnels. Yet they were of the opinion that there were other entrances.

The officers shared their assessment of what might be below. It was an underground city containing everything necessary for autonomous existence for many years. The expedition discovered an underground subway system, complete with rails. There was no soot on the ceiling of the tunnel. The walls contained rows of cables. The train was moved by electrical power. The expedition entered the tunnel, but not at its beginning. The tunnel began somewhere under the lake. Its other end was probably somewhere near the Oder River, to the west. Soviet field engineers discovered an underground crematorium. Most likely those who built this city were burned here.

As the expedition slowly and cautiously walked the tunnel in the direction of West Germany, they discovered dozens of tunnels to the right and left. Most of the tunnels were sealed off. What lay behind the sealed entrances? What sites, what sections of the underground SS city were hidden there? We still have no answers.

The area was dry for the most part. As they walked through the underground tunnel, the Soviets began to lose their sense of reality. The investigation of this huge underground city lying under the fields, rivers, and forests was for top experts, well equipped, with plenty of resources and time. Meanwhile the expedition estimated that the underground city of Regenwurmlager could extend for dozens of kilometers and continue under the Oder. What the final destination was, they had no idea.

The expedition went back, and some time later, the commander of the Northern Group of Forces, Col.-Gen. P. Maryakhin, arrived in Keszyca and personally descended into the underground SS city. I was not able to find out if he discovered anything of importance during his mission.

Liskin had determined that from 1958 to 1992, there had been nine commanders of the brigade, and each one of them had to get used to being a neighbor of the mysterious underground territory. One of the last commanders, V. Spiridonov, learned more about the Regenwurmlager. He was privy to reports of the field engineers, because most of the brigade's commanders considered it to be their duty to learn as much as possible about the SS city.

Spiridonov's Investigation

Spiridonov revealed that the area where the subway extended under the Oder was flooded. The distance between Keszyca and the Oder is 60 kilometers. The walls and ceiling of the subway system were covered with concrete plates, while the floor was covered with rectangular stone plates. Spiridonov himself drove 20 kilometers toward Germany in a Soviet military vehicle through the underground tunnel.

Stairs leading to a bunker and the outer air.

As he learned, the person who knew most about the city was a quiet Pole, Dr. Podbelsky of Miedzyrzecz, who at the end of the 1980s was about ninety years old. He had secretly explored the underground city in the 1940s and '50s. Dr. Podbelsky told local inhabitants that the city was first built by the Germans in 1927, but the really intensive construction began in 1933 after Hitler came to power.

In 1937, Hitler reportedly visited the Regenwurmlager himself, arriving by the underground subway. It was then that the city was turned over to the Wehrmacht and the SS. There were some secret passageways from the Regenwurmlager to the strategic underground storage places and a plant, located in the area of Visoka and Peski villages, some five kilometers from the lake (to the north and west of it).

Lake Keszyckie itself is a mystery to be solved. It is as deep as 20 meters in its eastern end, and it was there that sometimes in the summer, Soviet officers who were fishing in the lake could discern something in the murky bottom that looked like a hatch. They nicknamed it "Eye of the Inferno," and this eye seemed to be closed shut. What was the purpose of the hatch? Was it a Kingston valve to flood the underground city in case of an emergency? But if the city was not flooded, then it might have been kept intact for some other purpose and may contain unimaginable secrets.

Spiridonov found many intriguing sites around the lake and in the forest. Among them were pillboxes containing machine guns, surrounded by minefields, barbed wire, and deadly traps. He found ruins of military structures, remnants of the hospital for the SS elite forces.

But throughout the period of Soviet control of the territory, no comprehensive and detailed exploration of the Regenwurmlager had taken place.

Obviously, the Soviets and the Polish government at the time would attempt to limit access to the Regenwurmlager to prevent unauthorized movement to and from West Germany. To expect anything less from them would be highly naive, and yet there are no records that I know of to provide pertinent details about such Soviet security measures or actions.

The Regenwurmlager could contain hidden treasures, art pieces looted by Nazi invaders in occupied Europe. But it could also be that it holds a still undiscovered key to the German program to build an atomic bomb. Did the fleeing SS troops enter it to disappear in the bowels of the Earth? We do not know what the Polish government discovered after the Soviets departed, but it is unlikely that the Poles had many resources to explore the underground city.

The Other Regenwurmlager

I also received interesting information from France regarding another construction that involved a Regenwurmlager.

In 1943, the secret Nazi program of V1 and V2 rockets became a top priority because Germany was beginning to lose the war.

Nazi Germany built several fortified V2 rocket-launch sites in France. The most impressive and well-preserved ones are located in the northern part of the country. One was at Watten, in the Eperlecques Forest, the other

Part of the Regenwurmlager complex.

at Wizernes-Helfaut.

After the Allied bombing and damage to the Watten bunker site on August 27, 1943, the German Army looked to the quarry at Wizernes-Helfaut as an alternative prospect for V2 underground operations. Here, inside and around the old mining quarry, the Nazis began work in October 1943 on the second of several giant, hardened bunkers intended for launching forty to fifty V2 rockets at England on a daily basis.

The site at Wizernes-Helfaut is a tunnel complex built under an enormous concrete dome over a chalk quarry. Not far from Saint-Omer, one of the most imposing bunkers of the V2 project, the "Cupola," was built by the Todt organization. Actually, 1,300 abused, overworked, and humiliated workmen, slaves of Nazi Germany, built the site. The workers were young Frenchmen and Soviet prisoners of war of both sexes forced to work under the Nazis' Obligatory Service. After the project was abandoned in 1944, five hundred Soviet POWs were sent to Germany by train. No one knows what happened to them.

The Wizernes-Helfaut bunker received the code name of "Bauvorhaben 21, Schotterwerk Nord West."

Let us briefly compare the Polish and French Nazi-designed underground constructions. The dimensions of the dome were immense: seventy-one meters in diameter and five meters thick, weighing fifty-five thousand tons. A series of connecting tunnels (about seven kilometers of underground galleries) would be excavated beneath the dome and hillside.

The site plans included galleries dug in the chalky plate for storage of the rockets, the fuel supply, a liquid-oxygen production facility, housing for the garrison, and electrical generators. There were paths leading from outside, through rocket- height doors into the interior assembly area. Inside, the rockets could be serviced and assembled safely, shielded from Allied bombing by the massive dome and the chalk hill as well. A small railway supply tunnel led to all of the underground works and a large octagonal chamber more than 100 feet under the dome.

A special SS battery of V2 troops was planned to run the operations at the Cupola. German plans included building a V2 guidance bunker some eight kilometers south, at Roquetoire.

Other features of the Wizernes complex were to include the Regenwurmlager, code named "Frontlager Schotterwerk Nord West." Along with the building of the Wizernes dome complex for remotely firing V2s, the Germans built predefined locations for V2 mobile-launching units. These were regular mobile launch sites, thirty to fifty of them scattered across the countryside around Wizernes. They were called "Regenwurm Stellungen." Some of the concrete pads can still be found today. The prepared V2s were to come out from the Wizernes complex and parked in a planned (but never constructed) tunnel system called "Regenwurmlager" in the hills, on the left of the hospital.

Allied aircraft began dropping bombs on Wizernes-Helfaut in April 1944. Over time, they were able to cause heavy damage to the bunker regardless of very effective German flak batteries. The site was ultimately abandoned as a rocket base in August 1944, mainly as a result of the huge damage to the outside communication lines (roads and railway) that made further construction nearly impossible. The bunker was rendered useless by precise and deadly Allied bombing raids, and the Germans decided to abandon the site. It was the mobile launchers (Meilerwagen) that Nazis would use for their V2 rockets launched from occupied Western Europe.

Ultimately, a single rocket was launched from the nefarious Cupola. It was forgotten until after the British Army conducted an investigation in 1944. But nowadays the site has become a museum and contains a fascinating display of a V2 rocket and a display featuring the German secret weapons programs.

Epilogue?

What is the connection between the two Regenwurmlagers? What happened to the Totenkopfdivision SS forces in the Miedzyrzecki Fortified Region? What is hidden in the sealed tunnels in the underground SS city? Would there be some heretofore-undiscovered Nazi-looted artwork and treasures? Or some German secret weapons R&D projects? Has the city itself been "put on ice" for some future use? Did the Polish government know something sinister about the site, and plan to dump nuclear waste into the Regenwurmlager tunnels to render the underground SS city forever inaccessible?

So far we have only questions, but no answers.

Part Three
Mysteries of Time

Chapter 9

Ghost Trains of Eurasia

Among the odd phenomena that are found in Eastern Europe and Russia, ghost trains are definitely among the strangest. I have collected many reports of phantom trains, and I believe there are many more unreported cases, mainly due to the reluctance of railroad professionals to discuss such unexplained phenomena.

Eerie tales of ghost trains have appeared in Russian publications, including the *Trud* newspaper, *Tekhnika Molodezhi* magazine, and the *Sovershenno Sekretno* newspaper. A detailed article was featured on September 25, 1998, in *Rossiyaskaya Gazeta,* a publication of the Russian Federation government.

The phenomenon of the ghost train (*poyezd-prizrak,* in Russian) has also been studied by a group of scientists from Moscow State University.

Gogol's Skull

Nilolay A. Cherkashin, a retired Soviet naval officer, journalist, and philosopher, has collected a number of fascinating stories regarding the ghost train phenomenon. He has dedicated over fifteen years of his life to the research of the subject.

One of Cherkashin's more macabre stories concerns the missing skull of one of Russia's most celebrated writers.

Nikolay Gogol was born in Sorochintsi, Ukraine, in 1809 and grew up on his parent's country estate. His family's original surname was Yanovsky, but the novelist's grandfather had taken the name "Gogol" to claim a noble Cossack ancestry. Nikolay Gogol was a famous Russian short story writer, novelist, and playwright, called the "Russian Dickens" by many. His plays, short stories, and novels rank among the great masterpieces of nineteenth-century Russian realist literature. His books were full of unforgettable and often grotesque characters, eerie mysteries, and incredible occurrences.

Gogol died in 1852 (he was insane at the time of his death) and was buried at the cemetery of Moscow's Svyato Danilov (St. Daniel) Monastery.

Gogol once wrote: "I am destined by the mysterious powers to walk hand in hand with my strange heroes, viewing life in all its immensity as it rushes past me, viewing it through laughter seen by the world and tears unseen and unknown by it."

Gogol's life and death were full of strange occurrences. In his final years Gogol came under the influence of an obsessive priest, Father Konstantinovskii, and burned the sequels for his famous novel Dead Souls. That happened ten days before Gogol died from madness on March 4, 1852. The writer had refused to take any food, though various remedies were employed to make him eat: spirits were poured over his head, leeches attached to his nose, and hot loaves applied to his person. Some believe that Gogol was buried alive. A rumor circulated that when the Communists demolished the cemetery and Gogol's grave was opened, he was found lying on his side with the coffin's edging badly torn. Some in Moscow believe that Gogol was buried twice.

In 1931, during the early years of Stalin's regime, the Soviets moved Gogol's remains to Moscow's Novodevichye (New Maiden) Cemetery. The

Nikolay Gogol.

Danilov monastery was later turned into a juvenile prison, as the Marxist anti-religious campaigns engulfed Russia, and churches and synagogues were closed down or destroyed.

When Gogol was exhumed, the Soviet authorities found his body but no head.

Rumors attributed the theft of Gogol's skull to Alexey A. Bakhrushin (1865–1929). The latter distinguished himself as a collector of theatrical memorabilia; later in life, Bakhrushin became an accomplished theater historian and transformed his collection of relics into a treasury of national and world theater, which he donated to the city of Moscow. A successful businessman, Bakhrushin was an honorary member of the Imperial Academy of Sciences, a Moscow City Council Speaker, and one of the founders and leaders of the Russian Theatre Association. Allegedly, Bakhrushin had incited two watchmen of the monastery's necropolis to steal Gogol's skull in 1909. There were rumors that Bakhrushin also possessed the skull of M. Shchepkin (1788–1863) a famous Russian actor who worked on the stage of the Maly (Small) Theater.

These rumors reached Lieutenant Yanovsky, an officer of the Russian Imperial Navy and a relative of Nikolay Gogol. Yanovsky threatened to shoot Bakhrushin if Gogol's skull was not returned. The theater afficionado relented, and Yanovsky departed with a rosewood casket for Sevastopol, the Crimean port city where he served.

Not long after that, Italian Navy minelayers arrived in Sevastopol to take aboard the remains of some Sardinian generals for reburial. Yanovsky handed the casket to one of the Italian captains, asking him to deliver it to the Russian Counsel General.

In the spring of 1911 the Italian captain departed on a long voyage. His younger brother, a university student, embarked on a train with a group of his friends for a fun-filled journey. The student wanted to play a joke on his friends by scaring them when the train entered a very long tunnel. He took Gogol's skull with him to use as a prop in his practical joke. But just before the train entered the tunnel its passengers inexplicably panicked. The student decided to jump off the footboard. He later told reporters that a strange, viscous, white cloud had engulfed the unfortunate train. He described the inexplicable horror and panic felt by its passengers and confessed to taking the rosewood casket from his brother's study. Out of 106 passengers, only two were able to jump off before the train vanished inexplicably. The tunnel was later examined by local authorities, but they did not even find soot from the engine's smoke. The fateful tunnel's entrance was sealed; a bomb struck the tunnel during World War II.

Tarakanov's Research

Boris Tarakanov became interested in the story of the mysterious ghost train (or "The Flying Italian," as some call it). He contacted Italian colleagues, who conducted their own investigation. They learned that a train indeed disappeared in 1911. It was a three-cab train, rented for tourists by the Italian company Sanetti. There is a model of the train, some say, in storage at the Milan Railroad Museum. The investigators tried to find what had happened by studying the toy-like model, but to no avail.

In Mexico, Boris Tarakanov discovered a fascinating hint of the vanished train. About the time the train disappeared, papers of a famous Mexican psychiatrist were published dating to the 1840s. These papers mention the curious case of 104 Italians who spent a week in a Mexican psychiatric clinic because they claimed to have arrived in Mexico by train.

Do ghost trains travel through time and space?

Since the Italian train's disappearance, the skull of Nikolay Gogol has allegedly traveled throughout the world aboard the phantom locomotive. It has been sighted on several occasions in Zavalichi, the vicinity of Poltava,

Ukraine, in the area where the famous writer was born. In 1940, just before Adolf Hitler's birthday, the ghost train reportedly appeared on the top-secret single-track railroad leading to Hitler's headquarters. The eerie ghost train was also sighted in the railroad tunnel under La Manche.

Disappearance of 1991

Another appearance of Gogol's ghost train in 1991 in the Poltava region was noticed and reported in two Ukrainian newspapers, Pravda Ukrainy and Slava Sevastopolya on August 12, 1992. Yelena Chebrets, a monitor at the railroad crossing, confirmed that the train had appeared on September 25, 1991. On that day, V. P. Leschatiy, a scientist from Kiev and the chairman of the anomalous phenomena research commission of the Ukrainian Academy of Sciences, waited for the recurrent arrival of the ghost train at the crossing. When the poyezd-prizrak appeared from nowhere, he jumped into the last passing cab in front of several witnesses. The train vanished, along with the Ukrainian scientist, and the man has not been heard from since.

According to the newspaper *Forum*, the ghost train has been seen at the crossing after the incident more than once, but so far no one wants to try to board it. The same newspapers described the appearance of the ghost train in Crimea during Khruschev's rule (1955), in the area of Balaklava. There, the train passed over an old embankment from which the rails had been removed long ago.

URO and Scientists

Gogol's ghost train has been reported by witnesses in Moscow, Novosibirsk, Sakhalin Island, Karelia, and other cities and regions of the former Soviet Union and Eurasia. It has been invariably described as a steam engine of a non-Russian make, with an empty engineer's cabin, three cabs with closed window blinds, and some open doors.

Another term used by Russian railroads is neopoznanniy zheleznodorozhniy obyekt, or Unidentified Railroad Object (URO). UROs have been sighted, according to rumors, in the Moscow region and in the capital city itself in 1975, 1981, 1986, and 1992. Tarakanov conducted excellent research, but when he discussed the phenomenon with retired KGB officers, they quite seriously and confidentially advised him to be less interested in "all of this."

Physicist and mathematician Ivan P. Patsey, a docent of Moscow State University, heads a group of Russian scientists who have become interested in the phenomenon of ghost trains. The group includes a railroad expert and a philosopher along with people of other professional backgrounds. This organization has conducted field research around the large railway junctions of Baranovichi and Pskov, where Gogol's ghost train has been sighted.

Patsey theorizes that the railroads of Eurasia form the largest planetary structure created by human beings. This gigantic network of railroads has to have an influence on the flow of time. Patsey believes that any considerable transformation of space causes temporal anomalies. Time and space, with its electromagnetic properties, are inseparably linked. Patsey's expedition discovered a law of conservation of time: spent time does not disappear.

A Chronal Hole?

Patsey's group recalled the deadly Messina earthquake that took place in Italy on December 28, 1908, claiming approximately one hundred thousand lives. The 7.5-magnitude earthquake could have caused a huge crack in the chronal field. If this "wandering chronal hole" projected itself on the mountain tunnel, it could have moved Gogol's ghost train into some other space. Because the movement of the train was determined by hard spatial coordinates (railroad tracks), it could only appear where tracks had existed in the past, or where they would exist in the future.

Ukraine, 2002

Vyacheslav Fomenko, a TV operator in Zaporozhye, Ukraine, was coming home one Saturday from a fishing trip. About 11:00 a.m. he came to the

Plavni railroad station. Some fifty meters from the station he observed a train appearing from nowhere. The sudden appearance of six or seven antiquated train cabs baffled him. Where did they come from? There was no one at the station but Fomenko. The weather was clear. The train looked absolutely real. Fomenko became afraid. Then he heard the sound of train wheels: a freight train was approaching the ghost train on the same track. It seemed that a collision was about to take place. But several hundred meters before the impact, the ghost train disappeared into thin air. When Fomenko told the story to his colleagues, they laughed. But he insisted he was not drunk. He is of sound mind and not known for being a practical joker.

Ukraine, 1995

Later Fomenko learned of a very similar incident. On July 14, 1995, the head of the Kiev Psychiatric Hospital, Pavel Andreychenko, was attending to a very strange patient. Anton Gnatyuk was a forty-year old warrant officer and commander of a radar platoon. His story echoes the event observed by Fomenko.

Coming home from a trip, Gnatyuk purchased tickets for the train departing the next morning. But he had no money to stay at an inn, so he made arrangements with the train conductors to spend the night in one of the passenger cars stationed in the RIP tracks (a spur or siding with facilities for "Repair in Place" maintenance). There he found a strange train that looked to be of a pre-World War II construction. He decided to sleep inside one of its cabs. But when the warrant officer touched the handle of the door, he was knocked out by a powerful electrical shock. The train vanished into thin air. Gnatyuk barely survived the ordeal.

Unexplained Deaths

Novoye Obozreniye, a Siberian newspaper, published an article on February 27, 2002, about strange incidents involving Russian railroads.

A very unusual incident happened not far from Balakovka Village in the Vologda region. On September 15, 2001, a group of mushroom gatherers approached the rail tracks leading to an abandoned peat mine. Lying on the tracks was the torn body of a man. Several meters of the railroad ties were covered in blood. The impact was so great that the body was broken into pieces. Two women fainted after seeing the corpse.

When the official criminal investigation into the death of this Russian "John Doe" was opened, detectives were shocked to learn that the abandoned railroad branch line had not served any trains for 20 years. The ties were covered with rust, and overgrown with vegetation. The cause of death of the unknown man on the rail tracks has never been determined. One thing is clear: only a train traveling at great speed could have maimed the man to such an extent. The nearest working railroad is located twenty kilometers away. But if there were no trains on the abandoned branch line, what killed him?

A no less mysterious case happened three months earlier in the central Asian republic of Turkmenia.

Hamurat Berdiyev, the Minister of Turkmenian Rail Road Service, perished on June 14, 2001. He was only forty-one years old at the time. Although his death was strange, the Russian media ignored it. The only media mention besides that in Novoye Obozreniye was posted on a Turkmenian website.

Berdiyev was conducting an inspection close to the Ashkhabad Locomotive Depot. The official story is that the hapless minister failed to notice an approaching locomotive and perished under its wheels. But according to persistent rumors that have circulated ever since among Turkmenian railroad workers, the engineer of the train that ran over Berdiyev claimed that some "powerful force" brought down the minister before the locomotive reached him. The investigation of the Turkmenian Prosecutor General's office did not accept the engineer's testimony. Investigators also ignored the fact that the locomotive did not show any traces of the impact—no traces of blood, no fragments of clothing. Yet the autopsy determined that the minister died after being hit by a locomotive; his injuries corroborated that fact.

Invisible Waves

Thousands of people have perished in Russia and the former Soviet republics in railroad-related cases. Many of them die mysteriously, just as John Doe of Balakovka, or the Turkmen minister.

Seasoned Russian railroad professionals do not like to discuss such cases. One of them, Vladimir Donskoy, has thirty years of experience driving electric trains in the Moscow region. Six tragedies occurred during his long watch. Three were easily explained by consequences of alcohol consumption among Russian youths. But the other three he could neither explain nor forget.

When a person stands near the edge a railroad platform and a train races past him or her, it is easy to be sucked under the wheels by the vacuum. The moving train creates a vortex that sucks objects onto the track and under its wheels. Most of those pulled under have been standing in the front part of the platform, where the train is still moving at speed. They were always sucked under the second cab. Such are the laws of physics, according to Vladimir Donskoy, who saw three people pulled under the trains he was driving even before he reached the station. A person standing near the edge of the platform would be pushed back by a wave of heavy air. He or she tries to maintain equilibrium, pushing one leg downward, and thus pushes himself or herself under the train. Three such deaths personally observed by Donskoy convinced him that investigators from the Russian police were wrong to classify them as suicides. The detectives were very unhappy and clearly showed their mood to him after he visited relatives of the deceased and told them that what he saw was no suicide.

Vladimir Donskoy was concerned with the mystical aspect of the deaths and consulted other Russian locomotive engineers. All of them concurred that on occasion an invisible wave appears in front of the train at a distance of about seventy meters. The force of the wave is so powerful that it creates the impression of a ghostly locomotive moving in front of the train; a ghost train of sorts. The invisible train pulls people under.

Railroads are still among the safest means of transport, but some aspects of rail travel are not open to conventional explanations.

Chapter 10

Russia's Time Machine

Russian scientists have been experimenting with a machine that can physically alter time. Vadim Alexandrovich Chernobrov sent me the materials I used for writing this article. He and his colleagues have created a time machine that, although still limited, has enormous potential—and enormous dangers.

Chernobrov graduated from the Moscow Aviation Institute, where he studied at the Department of Astronautics and Automatic Flying Craft. His degree work and research thesis involved a project dealing with a promising space transport system (containing an unusual electromagnetic engine)—which can be transformed into a time machine. Besides his main work at the Moscow Aviation Institute, Chernobrov is also a science editor and a columnist for several Russian newspapers, including the prominent *Rossiyskiye Novosti*. He is also an engineer responsible for designing spacecraft, and since 1988 he has labored to create a UFO-like flying craft.

The time machine the Russians created is currently limited. It can only slow down or speed up time by four minutes in a twenty-four-hour period. Chernobrov hopes that in the future the machine will be able to move through time and space at much faster speeds. Because of many years spent on research, the Russian scientist is ever more certain that a part (but only a part) of all UFOs are vehicles for travel through time. He believes that in all probability they have arrived here from the future. Chernobrov mentions Albert Einstein's alleged secret calculations for the U.S. Navy experiments in 1943 (the so-called Philadelphia Experiment). The Russians believe that Enstein destroyed his manuscripts because he was afraid his ideas about time travel could be used to harm humanity. The Russians (including Chernobrov) are certain that Einstein's manuscripts contained mathematical substantiation that it is possible to travel to other dimensions and through time. There are also rumors of an electromagnetic field that the U.S. military allegedly used (based on Einstein's design) to create an invisible ship.

What method did Chernobrov use to alter time? He knew that neither chemical reactions, nor revolving flywheels, nor gravitational vortices were very promising. All these processes have a very limited effect on time. It is also almost impossible to control these processes. Therefore, Chernobrov rejected them in his attempt to create transport systems.

Instead, Chernobrov's theory explains time (a physical phenomenon), under certain conditions, as a manifestation of electromagnetic forces. It follows that with the help of such forces time could be influenced. A machine based on such theory can be easily controlled and might be able to provide higher performance.

The first model of the time machine was named "Lovondatr." It began functioning on April 8, 1988. The results were modest. The machine was created with volunteer aid from experts from the Moscow Aviation Institute, the Kbrunichev aerospace plant and scientific design bureaus Salyut and Energiya. Kbrunichev is now heavily involved in joint projects with American aerospace defense contractors.

From 1988 to 1993 four experimental time machines were created. All

Vadim Alexandrovich Chernobrov.

were lentil-shaped machines. They were constructed around a closed space that has special electromagnetic properties. Each also has a control unit, a power unit, and instrumentation. The needed electromagnetic fields configuration is created by a series of electromagnetic operating surfaces nested in each other under the *matryoshka* principle. (*Matryoshkas* are the Russian wooden dolls in peasant dresses that have successively smaller dolls fitted inside them.) These layers of flat electromagnets were twisted into an ellipsoidal shape. The outer layer was either attached to the power shell or was itself a power source. The operating conditions, specified by the control unit, could be diversified, and for each model of time machine it was possible to choose the most optimum frequency, tension, and switching-mode ratios. When Chernobrov was designing his promising space transport system based on time machine technology, he came to a conclusion that the most optimal shape for it would be that of a flying saucer.

The maximum value of the altered time was established inside the smallest *matryoshka*. During experiments, scientists observed, as expected, altered time outside the apparatus, too. Time measurements were taken with a pair of quartz generators and also with a standard clock, and precise time signal electronic and mechanical clocks placed in the payload section duplicated readings. The first time machine had a difference in readings of up to one half-second an hour, while subsequent, modified machines showed a time difference of up to forty seconds an hour.

The volume of payload in the center of the time machine was about that of a soccer ball. Therefore, dogs, the traditional pioneer travelers, were not used. The honor belonged to mice. The first experiments, which transported insects and mice into the past, killed the experimental animals, despite the time difference being only two seconds. Those humans who were not careful and stood too close to the time machine during the experiment developed symptoms of disease, analogous to those developed by American sailors who participated in the Philadelphia Experiment. After the layout of the machine was improved, the animal test pilots survived the process of transporting them through time. Chernobrov believes that humans will be able to travel through time by the beginning of the next century.

The first experiments with the time machine have slightly raised the curtain that shrouds the mystery of time. According to the preliminary data, time has many measures: It is heterogeneous and changeable. The present is but a passage of the multivaried future (the crown of the tree) into the mono-varied past (the tree trunk). Travel into the future is possible only through one branch, but the return to the present is possible through any of the branches, because they will all return the time machine to the primordial point.

Travel into the past guarantees that the time machine will come to any event that has occurred. And if the visit does not result in undesirable contacts and the movement of history is not altered, the return to the starting line should be unhindered. Otherwise, the return will take place through another branch, but the movement of history will change only for the time travelers. They will not be able to get to the point from which they started and will find themselves in another version of the present—that is, in a parallel world.

Chernobrov understands what drove Albert Einstein to destroy his manuscripts. In a world where there are wars, a time machine can be turned into a super weapon. Here is an example: We know that the force of destruction of any explosive depends on the velocity of percussion. If we place the charge into the capsule where time flows differently, then we can create a high-explosive bomb from a simple grenade. What if we use an atomic bomb instead of a grenade? A time machine is a superb means of transportation—it is elusive, and no aircraft, no rocket can compare with it.

Chernobrov is certain that although Einstein burned his manuscripts, the ideas that the great scientist developed could not be burned away. No direction in science can be blocked. What Chernobrov is concerned about is making sure that evil does not come from such ideas. He has closely watched the work of other specialists who want to open the mystery of time. These experts have approached the problem from many directions, but are walking the right path. Not long ago Chernobrov found alarming reports about scientific research into certain high-temperature semiconductors—no true time machine could be created without them. Then these reports stopped appearing in the international press, as if the scientists had been silenced. Chernobrov thinks the answer lies with the military. The military has made this subject classified.

This alarms the Russian scientist because of the time machine's potential to become a terrible super weapon. Chernobrov calls upon all experts involved in the development of time machines to participate in international, peaceful cooperation.

But perhaps Chernobrov should look no farther then his own backyard. The Russian newspaper *Trud* published a report in its July 30, 1992, issue about a flying saucer-like aircraft that underwent successful test flights. The craft was created and built at a military-industrial facility by experts from the experimental mechanical engineering design bureau. The apparatus's movement is based on the following principle: A high temperature superconductor travels about and is exposed to the rapid flow electrons. The report in *Trud* tells us that the Russian military has come close to creating a time machine of its own. It means that the creation of a real, usable time machine is not far off.

Chapter 11

Mysterious Gastropods

According to a very old Chinese legend, two giant red snails once lived on the hill behind a temple. The snails emitted strange lights at night. Because of that they were worshiped by local villagers. Later, the mountain was renamed Red Snail Hill and the temple Red Snail Temple (Hong Luo Si). Originally the temple was called Great Brightness Temple when it was built in A.D. 348. Today a scenic spot, the Red Snail Temple is located in the Huai Rou County northeast of Beijing. What paranormal properties did the gigantic snails possess? Snails have been observed to possess unusual properties in lands located far away from China throughout recorded history.

Snails have been on this planet longer than the primates; they appear in the fossil record around five hudred million years ago. There are around eighty thousand species of snails that have been identified today; most can be found in the marine environment. They, a part of the *Mollusca* phyllum, the *Gastropoda* class ("stomach foot," because they crawl on their stomach), a huge group of animals that has adapted to most habitats on Earth. Gastropoda are distinguished by their having a single shell.

Did Snails Build Pyramids?

When the Spanish conquistadors invaded areas of Central America and Mexico in the sixteenth century, they discovered the ruins of the great Mayan civilization. The Maya vanished and left evidence of their lost grandeur in massive structures in the surrounding rain forest. From A.D. 300 to 900, Mayan civilization had highly accurate calendars, mathematics, hieroglyphic writing, and a complex social and political order—and mysterious building techniques. Deep within the jungles of Mexico and Guatemala and extending into the Yucatán peninsula remain the fabled temples and palaces of the Maya. An article published in Russian magazine *Neveroytaniy Mir* in 2004 discussed ancient snails of Central and South America. Its author, Vladimir Kulakov, mentioned an archaeological discovery in a Mayan burial chamber of an important priest.

Among other artifacts discovered were very dirty leather bags. No one paid close attention to the bags, assuming that the contents must have spoiled ages ago. The archaeologists were more interested in finding tangible treasures, decorations, and art objects of the vanished civilization. The bags were considered to be ritualistic objects, containing food or drink for the departed. The contents were actually of a liquid nature, sticky, with very unusual smell. Someone had torn one of the bags and having determined that its contents were of no value, dropped the bag on the stone floor. The slimy contents oozed out and spilled all over the chamber's floor. No one paid attention to it until they came back in the morning and discovered that the floor had become soft. One could model it, like clay, and make shapes from it. Kulakov believes that the bags contained the most valuable item that the priest wanted to take with him to the afterlife. Turning rocks into soft dough, the priest possessed an uncanny ability, perhaps the ability to build the very complex Mayan structures that astound the researchers today.

Perhaps this lost secret of a vanished civilization can explain how the gigantic edifices of the lost civilizations were built, for example the Baalbek acropolis in the Middle East. This discovery would change our views on the technologies used by ancient builders. Perhaps they had special vessels where the mysterious "slime" was kept and deposited rocks and stones into it. When the contents became soft, the builders carried it to the construction sites where it was used for foundations and walls. That would enable the ancient Maya to build the gigantic structures in the first millennium. Our modern concrete is a compound of sand, gravel, and cement. The cement is a mixture of various minerals which, when mixed with water, hydrate and rapidly become hard, binding the sand and gravel into a solid mass. But the "slime" found in the Mayan burial chamber was a different compound, and if used to build the ancient, wonderful structures that stand erect thousands of years later, unlike modern buildings, one can see a clear difference. Kulakov believes that the explanation of the nature of the "slime" (alas, long lost) can be found by studying snails in aquariums. The Maya, without advantage of metal tools, beasts of burden, or even the wheel were able to construct vast cities with an astonishing degree of architectural perfection and variety. Perhaps they used other, albeit unusual, means.

Shell Building

Snails consume debris and algae in the aquarium. Among the items consumed is calcium. Somehow the snails are able to devour the debris and build their shells. Perhaps the ancient architects used the snails in their technology to create the long-forgotten "slime" that softens stones. Perhaps there existed another species of the snails, now extinct. There are many species of snails in the marine environment of Mesoamerica, surrounded by the Pacific, the Mexican Gulf, and the Caribbean. Perhaps the builders of the ancient world were able to discover the secret of the gastropods and adapted and applied it in the technology, allowing them to build the Mayan pyramids and large-scale structures more than one thousand years ago, not to

Trumpet snail.

mention other mysterious ancient structures.

Kulakov presents an interesting hypothesis. Let us look at some modern gastropods. Trumpet snails rarely eat plants; they forage around in the substrate and cling to the glass of the tank, eating the debris and thus cleaning the aquarium. Cerith snails, also glass cleaners, devour algae and diatoms; and then there is the Mexican Nerite, which eats the algae and diatoms both from the rocks and the glass and does not leave an algae film on the glass.

The shell and the tissue which makes it (the mantle) are distinctive features of animals in the phylum *Mollusca*. The snail's shell is usually coiled and is a part of the snail's living body. The soft-bodied section of the snail can be withdrawn into the shell, forming a defense against predators. The shell of the snail is largely calcium carbonate. They also contain small amounts of protein, but in reality the composition is more complicated and may depend on several factors. Generally, it is a complex structure consisting of many different layers. What is quite interesting is that snails that belong to different species and inhabit the same area still have different contents of bind calcium in their shells.

According to *Science Daily* (October 31, 2007), German scientists have recently discovered that the shells of some land snails carry an additional camouflage layer consisting of soil and have mountains of bizarre protuberances. *Napaeus barquini*, a snail from the Canaries, produces its impressive camouflage layer by itself in the process of an unexpectedly complex behavioral pattern: it grazes lichen material from the substrate and applies it to the surface of its shell with its mouth. The snail extends its body far beyond its shell margin and deposits the lichen material in the farthest areas of the shell.

When snails find food, they use their grate-like tongue, located under the tentacles, to shred it as a saw would. Some snails can grow their shell very fast. When a snail grows, the shell also must be enlarged to fit the snail's body. A snail extends its shell by adding new parts at the shell opening. The shell material is secreted by specialized cells of the mantle: first a transparent and thin organic outer layer is created, and then the calcified inner layers are deposited.

How did the Maya (and other ancient builders) build their temples and pyramids, and what were their primary reasons for using such construction techniques? It is feasible that the ancient sages had a different way to build their structures by using Nature; in this case, they used the snail's process of creating building materials for its shells to make hard rocks into a substance that could be transported and used for building complex structures. We already know of the Indian Ocean snail that that uses iron sulfides for structural purposes.

Medieval Instant Gastropod Messaging

Catharism, a dualist religion from Bulgaria, was introduced in Western Europe in the twelfth century. The Cathars condemned matter and flesh as evil and therefore rejected the Christian resurrection. They also denounced the wealth and the corruption of the Roman Catholic (*katharos* means "pure" in ancient Greek). The popularity of the Cathars in the Toulouse area and northern Italy scared Pope Innocent III, and he called for a Crusade in 1208. The "heretic" state of Languedoc was besieged, and a cruel, horrifying war ensued. It took the Crusaders almost sixty years to defeat the Albigenses. The Albigensian Crusade was against the people of the Languedoc in southern France. It is also known as the Cathar Crusade. Albigenses took their name from the town of Albi.

The Crusades ended in 1244 with the fall of the Château of Montségur. though Cathars were still being burned alive in the fourteenth century. The Inquisition was founded to exterminate the last vestiges of Cathar belief.

Relatively little is known about the Albigensian beliefs, since the sect was repressed and most evidence destroyed by inquisitors and their allies.

Well-known Russian writer and historian Nikolay N. Nepomnyaschiy, in his book *XX vek: otkritiye za otkritiyem* (2003) wrote about the remaining documents of the period that contain information regarding a mysterious abilities of the Albigensian leaders to communicate instantaneously and guide battles against the invaders. The secret of the Cathar "instant messaging" was partially uncovered when a French doctor, Henri Fabricius, published an article in the mid-nineteenth century about "biological telepathy." He claimed to be a descendant of one of those four Cathars who were able to leave the doomed Montsegur Castle through a secret underground passage. Working in the ruins of the castle, Dr. Fabricius had found documents of the long-gone days of the Cathar resistance. One document contained a detailed description of the "telegraph" used by the Cathars to communicate between their castles and fortresses. The crusade against the people of the Languedoc was one of sieges rather than open battles.

Medieval towns were generally surrounded by defensive walls, just like castles. Indeed, there is little distinction between castles and fortified towns in the Western Europe of the epoch.

A special pair of snails was used to transmit and receive information. The pair would be separated. One would be placed in the transmitting station while the other was taken to the receiving station. A special team of observers was stationed there around the clock. When the snail became agitated, it would be placed in a special groove with walls that had images of the Latin alphabet. When the snail stopped at a certain letter, the team would record that letter. Letters were made into words. The snail at the transmitting station was pricked with a pin and then placed in the similar groove. When the snail reached a certain letter, it was pricked again. It stopped, and at the same time its "sister" at a distance of many miles stopped also.

According to *Nepomnyaschiy*, another article about a similar ability of snails was authored by Hugo Zeitman and published in 1878. And in 1933, a newspaper in Berlin, Germany, published an article about experiments conducted on snails. The male species were placed on the white squares of a chessboard in one room while the females were placed on the same squares of a chessboard in another room up to eight hundred kilometers away. As soon as the males were moved to the black squares, the females in the other room, located far away, also moved to black squares on their own.

Gastropod Farmers, Armored Depth Dwellers, and Promising Painkillers

According to *Nature News* (Dececmber 2, 2003), *Littoraria irrorata* snails raise fungus on grasses so that they have a continuous food supply. They chew grass to prepare it for cultivation. Then they defecate on the chewed-up blades to fertilize their crop. The snails return to the wound and eat the fungus that grew in it. Does this fungal injection into plants prove that their intelligence is akin to that of human mushroom farmers?

According to *National Geographic News* (November 7, 2003), Swedish and American scientists have discovered a unique snail that has metal-plated armor on its body and on the underside of its foot. The as-yet-unnamed creature bears a mass of interlocking, iron-based plates on its body and the base of its foot. This unusual gastropod lives in the Indian Ocean near the Kairei hydrothermal vent. The scientists referred to it as a "very strange little beast" and the first animal discovered that uses iron sulfides for a structural purpose.

I have already discussed the fascinating and anomalous world of the black smokers, those underwater mineral "geysers." Hydrothermal vents are fractures in the Earth's surface where geothermally heated water pulses through. Usually, a hydrothermal vent is found where hot magma is close to the surface crust, as in volcanically active locations. This is where the yet-to-be-named snail lives. Black smokers eject high-temperature, dark water that was once trapped in molten rock beneath the Earth's crust. The water pressure is very high at the depths at which these vents occur, so the superheated water does not boil. Cooler currents near black geysers are rich in minerals and provide the iron sulfide compounds that the snails use in their metallic scales.

American scientists have been studying another very unusual gastropod. A snail that lives near coral reefs contains a chemical poison that might be useful as a pain killer. Studies have shown that the poison might be even stronger than morphine in relieving pain, according to the information published on *www.coralfilm.com/about.html.* Medicines derived from the chemical structure of the poison may have great potential for patients suffering from severe pain.

According to Wendy Wolfson's article in *InformationWeek* (January 28, 2002), researchers at the Max Planck Institute for Biochemistry in Munich have completed experiments to develop the first snail chip. They directly interfaced a neural network with a silicon semiconductor by growing snail synopses over the chip. When stimulated, the interlaced snail nerve cells transmitted electric pulses to trip a switch and make the circuit go live. German scientists plan to build a system with fifteen thousand neuron-transistor sites on the road to an eventual computational model of brain activity. Apparently, because neural cells from snails are somewhat larger than human, they are easier to see and manipulate.

Richard Satterlie, an American neurobiologist, has conducted scientific studies of a swimming snail at the Arizona State University, according to James Hathaway's 2002 article published at the university. He and his colleagues have learned that snail nerves are organized in groups that control certain functions, or "circuits," and that these circuit modules combine to work with other circuits and sometimes take on sharply different functions, depending on what other circuits they are working with. This leads to a neurophysiologic understanding of complex behavior.

The snails are known to be very well adapted to their environment. Their soft and flexible feet adapt to any surface. Thc negative pressure exerted by the foot sole allows the snail to crawl in any position, even with its shell down. The best known sense of a snail is its tactile sense. The snail's static sense (position) enables it to recover a normal position of the shell protecting its body after it is turned over.

Some day we will find out about other wonderful, perhaps paranormal, properties of the gatropods and put such to good use.

Part Four
Mysterious Russia

Chapter 12

An Interview with Russian Vampires

Once a week ten people gather in Alexy Vladimirovich's apartment in Vladivostok, Russia. What brings them together is their passion for blood. It matters not whose blood—most often it is bird blood. Those who gather at Alexy's apartment catch birds on their balconies with the help of elaborate traps. A bird is killed at the sacrificial table and its blood is poured into tiny liqueur glasses. Then the participants drink it. After the feast there is usually an hour-long exchange of opinions and idle talk, and then the guests leave.

Recently, a young lady approached Alexander Rempel, an anomalous phenomena researcher, at a Vladivostok Ufological Association meeting. Vampires had been discussed during the meeting. The information discussed was all derived from old books. The young woman took Alexander aside and informed him that such information was nonsense. She invited him to a real vampire meeting.

This is how Rempel found his way to Alexy Viadimirovich's apartment.

Once inside, Rempel noticed curtain-shrouded windows, silver candlesticks, a sacrificial table, and a metal tray with miniature crystal glasses. One of the men cut the head off a captured pigeon and collected the blood in a wide-rimmed goblet. Later, two more birds were sacrificed. Each vampire got his or her share of blood. When the ritual was over, Alexander was allowed to ask questions.

"What about human blood? What about all of those horrors described in various books dealing with vampires?"

One guest responded, "I suppose the horrors and passions described in such books did take place. Previously, a vampire had to conceal his or her peculiarity for fear of death. Unable to wait, the vampires would attack any suitable victim. Apparently, ancient vampires didn't know that the blood of animals and birds can delay the approach of vontile, a condition that affects vampires. When the condition sets in, the only thought that rules the mind of the vampire is how to find blood."

"Do you use only the blood of animals and birds?" Alexander asked.

"We try blood from various birds and animals, but once every two or three months one of us shares his or her own blood with the group."

"How does it occur?"

"Without any horrors. We neither bite into veins nor cut our fingers. It is absolutely harmless and painless to give one hundred grams of one's blood once a year for the ritual."

"Can you do without human blood?"

"What kind of vampires would we be then? We would be bloodsuckers. If we do not consume human blood for a long period of time a depression sets in, fevers develop, and some of us get convulsions. Avian blood delays these conditions, but we need human blood at least every three or four months."

"Then vampirism is a sickness?"

"For us blood is what insulin is for diabetics."

"Has the need for blood increased?"

"No. Previously we needed more blood, whereas now two or three sips are sufficient."

"Can the denizens of Vladivostok rest assured that you will not suck the blood of innocent victims?"

"We are ready to commit ourselves to it." As Alexander left the vampire's apartment, he was convinced that these were adults playing a childish game. The desire to be among the "chosen" can lead to a farfetched psychological dependence. In this case, it is dependence on blood.

Chapter 13

Echoes of the Sun

Alexander Chizhevsky (1897–1964) was an outstanding Russian thinker, a giant of his country's science, and a Soviet gulag prisoner. He was the founder of heliobiology, studying the influence of solar activity on biological and social processes and psychic powers, and worked in the areas of experimental biophysics and hematology. He also wrote poetry and literary criticism and taught history and archeology. His unpublished manuscripts are kept in the Archives of the Russian Academy.

Chizhevsky described life on Earth as "an echo of the Sun." The Sun, our nearest star, contains approximately 99.8 percent of the mass in the solar system, and has the strongest thermal, electromagnetic, and gravitational influence on our planet. Chizhevsky found many links between sunspot activity and general health issues. He made intensive studies of the correlation between solar-induced changes in the Earth's magnetic field and the occurrence of physical events, such as epidemics of cholera, diphtheria, typhus, and smallpox. He also firmly believed that signs of human unrest or "mass excitement," such as revolutions and mass migrations, followed the sunspot cycle.

Using immense historical and statistical material, Chizhevsky showed that solar activity acts as an accelerator and moderator upon the whole biosphere, which manifests in the frequency and magnitude of events of population growth and decline: births, deaths, harvests, heart attacks, emergencies, bank crashes, catastrophes, suicides, and more. This is a result of the reaction of the planet's core to changes in the electromagnetic corona of the Sun.

Chizhevsky collected data from seventy-two countries from 600 B.C. onward. Because of his research, more is known today about the phenomenon of the geomagnetic field and its influence on biological processes.

Chizhevsky's Chandelier

Another one of Chizhevsky's discoveries was very important. It had been previously been known that an animal or human may suffocate to death even when there is enough oxygen in the air if something elusive is absent from it. Chizhevsky identified this mysterious substance in the early 1920s. He proved that when the concentration of negatively charged aero-ions (known now as superoxide anion radicals) becomes much lower than one thousand ions per milliliter of air, oxygen molecules are poorly utilized by the organism. And if the net concentration of positively charged aero-ions exceeds that of negative ions, a quick death by suffocation can follow.

Devices based on this discovery were sold in a number of countries at the end of 1930s. Instead of light, the "Chizhevsky Chandelier" radiated a stream of electrons that joined to oxygen molecules, forming negatively charged oxygen ions.

Russian Cosmism

Chizhevsky belonged to the school known as Russian Cosmism, whose practitioners used both theoretical inquiry and empirical research to explore the history and philosophy of the origin, evolution, and future existence of the universe and humankind. Cosmism drew from both Eastern and Western philosophic traditions. Among its adherents were religious thinkers, philosophers, physical scientists, artists, and poets. Their global approach generated new fields of biological and social study, such as exobiology, biophysics, planetary ecology, geomagnetic biology, and ecological psychology or the psychology of life environment.

Russian Cosmism proposes that there is a common evolution of the biosphere and humanity. This notion became a secret impetus for pioneers of the Soviet space program like Konstantin Tsiolkovsky, who believed that Earth is the cradle for humankind and that sooner or later we will certainly move into space.

Geologist and biochemist Vladimir Vernadsky was a leading light of Russian Cosmism. He invented the concept of the biosphere in 1917, and in 1924 introduced the notion of the noosphere.

In 1917, the Marxist-Leninists grabbed control over Russia and Russian Cosmism was banned. Its practitioners were imprisoned or killed, and the philosophy was largely forgotten. Tsiolkovsky, the proponent of space flight and migration to other planets, was fortunate in that he continued his research and writings, and one can see some of the Russian Cosmist's idealism in Russia's Star City and the Gagarin Cosmonaut Training Center.

Chizhevsky experienced the heavy hand of Communist ideologues to the fullest degree. He was not afraid to defend astrology, and wrote that modern scientific discoveries actually bring us back to the knowledge of ancient Middle East. In 1929 he was invited to be a lecturer in biophysics at Columbia University in New York, and also became a member of the French Toulon Academy of Sciences.

The Soviet government supported Chizhevsky's research, but could not forgive his independent thinking. He was called a pseudoscientist and a charlatan, and in 1936 the newspaper *Pravda* dubbed him "an arrogant and false professor."

In 1939, Chizhevsky was elected president of the first International Biophysical Congress in New York, and was nominated for the Nobel Prize. But the Kremlin would not allow him to travel to the United States. In 1942, Chizhevsky was arrested, and he spent the next sixteen years in concentration camps, prisons, and exile. He was finally allowed to return to Moscow in 1958, long after Stalin had died. The brave Russian scientist passed away in 1964.

Alexander Chizhevsky.

In 1965, the Soviet Academy of Sciences realized the loss they had suffered and created a special commission for full-scale research of Chizhevsky's archives. A small star was named in his honor long after his death (3113 Chizhevsky). Who remembers those who persecuted him?

The Changing World

Chizhevsky's ideas about the impact of solar energy on the Earth are especially important now. Global warming is but one of the changes our planet is going through. If we pay heed to Chizhevsky's ideas, we might understand that increases in solar activity create a corresponding growth in the Earth's cataclysmic events. Earthquakes, droughts, wildfires, the melting of the polar icecaps, volcanic activity, hurricanes, and tornadoes are just some manifestations of the Sun's influence. All of them are on the increase. And our Earth is not the only planet of the solar system undergoing such changes. Our knowledge of the structure of the Sun is incomplete, and much of our present knowledge has been discovered very recently. Chizhevsky never believed that his research projects were finalized. There may be more discoveries in store for us.

Chapter 14

Mysteries of Russia's Greatest Psychic and Telepath

The human brain is mysterious, and its complex cognitive powers are far from being understood. In the darkest years of the turbulent twentieth century there lived a man who harnessed the mysterious powers of the brain like no other human being known to history. He was a telepath, a mind reader, a psychic, a remote viewer, and a lucky survivor who avoided both the Holocaust and the death camps of Joseph Stalin. We may never know the full extent of his extraordinary abilities.

Wolf Grigorievich Messing was born in 1899 to a poor Jewish family in the tiny town of Gora-Kavaleriya near Warsaw, in what was then part of the Russian Empire. As a young child he suffered from "lunatism," a disorder believed to be caused by the phases of the Moon. Messing was cured when his parents placed a tub of cold water by his bed, so he would step into it and wake up.

At the age of six Messing was sent to a religious school, where he distinguished himself by his devotion and his incredible ability to memorize prayers. Later he was enrolled in a yeshiva, but ran away after two years. Messing got on the first passenger train he could find, hid under a bench, and fell asleep. When the train conductor demanded his ticket, Messing picked a piece of paper off the floor and handed it to the man, looking into his eyes and willing that the man believe the scrap to be a genuine train ticket. He was successful, and arrived in Berlin with no further problems.

A Starving Medium

Messing was paid a pittance for menial work, and once fainted from hunger right on the street. He was taken to a morgue, where he was saved from his lethargy by the famous psychiatrist and neurologist Professor Abel. This man was the first to realize Messing's incredible mental powers and his ability to control his body. Abel began to conduct mind-reading experiments with the boy.

Messing could become cataleptic (entering a trancelike or unresponsive state of consciousness) at will. Later he found out that he could foretell the future in this state. Meanwhile, young Wolf began to work in the Berlin Panopticum (a circus) and a variety theater.

The professor was amazed with results of his experiments. Messing immediately understood all mental commands and executed them with precision. He trained himself by going to the Berlin market to read the minds of the vendors.

Abel also taught the teenager to turn off his feelings of physical pain. Messing became a fakir, and to supplement his income (and send money to his impoverished family), he let people pierce his chest and neck with nails in front of an audience.

International Fame

When he turned sixteen, Messing began his first tour, traveling to the city of Vienna. But he was no longer a circus attraction. Messing had developed

Wolf Grigorievich Messing.

a program of psychological experiments, as he modestly refered to them. During these "experiments" the teenager would execute commands sent to him mentally, tell biographies of people he never met before, and find items hidden by the audience.

Messing's growing fame attracted the attention of Albert Einstein. The great physicist invited the talented youth to his home, where Messing met Sigmund Freud. The psychologist immediately began his own mental experiments. He gave a mental command to young Wolf to get a pair of tweezers and pluck three hairs from Einstein's fabulous mustache. The youth did as he was instructed, albeit with embarrassment. But Einstein told him to turn to him for assistance, should he ever need it.

Messing never met with Einstein again, but learned from Freud the art of concentration and self-hypnotism. Later in his life Messing met with other famous people, including Gandhi in 1927.

In 1917, Messing began a world tour, amazing people throughout the planet. His circus days were over. In 1921 he returned to Poland, now a free country, and served in the army. Later, the now-famous young man toured the world again, with a renowned medium as his manager. He had enemies among charlatans who preyed on naïve people and their beliefs; they tried to compromise the psychic, but he knew of their plans through his incredible powers of perception. Messing also solved crimes and found lost valuables.

Enemy of the Third Reich

In 1937 Wolf Messing incurred the wrath of the demented Adolf Hitler. While performing in a Warsaw theater, the telepath foretold Hitler's demise if the Germans attacked Soviet Russia. Hitler was fascinated by mystical ideas, and reacted immediately and hysterically. The Nazis put a price of two hundred thousand Reichsmarks on Messing's head.

It is not clear whether Hitler wanted to murder Messing or to harness his powers in captivity. (His other famed psychic, Hanussen, an influential confidant of the superstitious Führer, was murdered in a Nazi power struggle.) Messing had to hide for a long time to evade the Germans.

After 1939, Nazi-occupied Warsaw was plastered with leaflets offering a reward for Messing's capture. On one occasion, he wandered carelessly on a busy city street where he was arrested and savagely beaten. At the police station, he collected all his mental strength and willed the guards to come to his cell. As they staggered inside, Messing left it, locked them in, and escaped. He left Warsaw through the sewer tunnels, hiding in a cart covered with hay, and made his way (traveling only at night, with trusted guides) to the Soviet Union. He crossed the Bug River in November 1939.

Stalin's Cunning Fellow

Messing handed the Soviets a Nazi leaflet that promised a reward for his capture. A Jewish refugee with strange talents, he did not find work immediately. He was lucky not to be sent to the gulag concentration camps. Later, Messing was protected by Panteleymon Ponomarenko, the Communist leader of the Byelorussian Republic, and allowed to perform. Soon thereafter the NKVD (secret police) interrupted his performances and dispatched the psychic to Moscow to meet the formidable Soviet leader.

Stalin became quite interested in Messing. Though he was not a religious believer, he did consider paranormal abilities to be a possibility. Stalin tested the extraordinary refugee by ordering him to rob a bank.

Shortly thereafter, Messing, followed by a squad of police officers, walked into the Central Bank headquarters in Moscow with an order to take away one hundred thousand rubles. Walking up to the teller's window, Messing handed him a blank sheet of paper and opened his briefcase. The teller was given a mental order, which he followed immediately and correctly, enthusiastically producing the required sum. Messing left the building with the money, but then immediately came back and gave the money back to the teller. The poor man looked at a blank piece of paper and the stacks of bills, and suffered a heart attack. Messing was happy to learn that the man survived.

Stalin was convinced. Fame came immediately; Messing became something of a superstar, and his success brought incredible income to the government. Messing's assistant, Valentina Ivanovskaya, recalled that the medium met with Stalin, Beria, Voroshilov, Kalinin, and other Soviet leaders. Once Stalin told him, "What a cunning fellow you are, Messing!" to which the telepath replied in less-than-perfect Russian: "It is not I who is the cunning one; it is you who is truly cunning!"

Kalinin nervously pulled his sleeve, but Stalin was obviously in a good mood that day. Perhaps Messing read the dictator's mind.

Stalin and Lavrenti Beria (head of the secret police) decided to test the hypnotist's abilities again. They asked if he could exit the Kremlin without a pass if the guards were warned not to let him out. Messing replied that he could. And he did leave the building without any problems, although a secretary followed him. No one stopped the medium, and he waved to the Soviet leaders from the street. The guards swore that the man who walked out past them was none other Stalin himself.

When Messing walked back into the building (as he recalled in his interview to Leningradskaya Pravda newspaper in 1964), the watch commander sent a message in his mind: "You dirty Yid!" The telepath struck him on the cheek with his own thought. And the officer jumped back.

The psychic consulted both Stalin and the chief of the NKVD on a number of occasions. Other meetings with the top party and secret police officials took place, and Messing suffered much stress as a result.

Aiding the War Effort

Messing did not perform from 1943 until the end of the war, allegedly because the Soviet government sent him on a mission to Siberia where he was placed in charge of an espionage college. But this period of his life has not been covered in his memoirs, and remains a mystery.

Not long before the Nazis invaded Soviet Russia, Messing was invited to speak with top Red Army commanders. He predicted that there would be a massive war with Germany, but it would end between May 3 and 5, 1945, with a Soviet victory. Stalin was informed about this prediction, and when the war ended, the Soviet dictator sent a congratulatory telegram to Messing. He kept the telegram for years.

Messing donated his own money for the construction of two military aircraft during the war, and helped his adopted country in many other ways. His family perished in the Holocaust.

A recently aired Russian television special implied that the famous psychic met Stalin some twenty hours before the dictator's death, and predicted that he would die soon. Messing initiated the meeting, as he wanted to intervene with Stalin on behalf of the doctors arrested in the infamous "Doctors' Plot" (in which a circle of Jewish physicians were accused of conspiring to poison senior Soviet leaders, including the dictator; some historians allege the plot was orchestrated by Stalin to justify a new purge of the party and the police and to prepare the country for a war with the West). Stalin warned Messing that he would be sent to the gulag if he did not stop meddling. After his death, Stalin's heirs quashed the accusations against the doctors and instead arrested and executed Beria; Messing could have predicted as much.

Some have noted that Stalin's death in March 1953 coincided with the holiday of Purim, and the implication is that the Jewish psychic removed the evil tyrant. But Messing was no murderer, and he did not play a role in the blood sport of Soviet politics. Otherwise, he would not have lived a long life in his adopted country. Curiously, another Russian television film about Messing was aired right after the first one, and made it quite clear that no such meeting ever took place. It looked like someone in Russia was trying to blame Stalin's death on the Jewish refugee who was given a haven in the USSR, yet there are those who protect Messing's name and honor.

Promotional poster for Wolf Messing.

Soviet Medium

During the war, the famous telepath gave many performances in the Soviet military units, military hospitals, and defense plants. His demonstration of mysterious qualities of human psyche and brain irked Communist ideologues and their materialistic propaganda. Before every performance after 1950, a statement from the Institute of Philosophy of the Soviet Academy of Sciences had to be read to the public announcing that Messing's abilities to read others' minds were based on "reflection of thoughts on motor human controls"—that is, he guessed the thoughts of others based on their involuntary and unconscious movements. Telepathy does not exist, proclaimed the so-called scientists, because Marxism-Leninism did not provide the guidelines as to its existence. A human thought cannot exist outside of the brain or the material world, and Messing's experiments had nothing to do with telepathy—this was the official ideological line.

Messing did not like to perform in big cities because he did not like to attract too much attention from the Communist leaders. But the Soviet people loved Messing's performances and filled the theaters whenever he was in town.

Once while performing in Kiev in the late 1940s, he was detained and brought to Moscow because Nikolay Bulganin, a top Soviet official at the time, had been ordered by Stalin to find a lost briefcase with top-secret documents. Messing was brought to the office of the individual who had lost the briefcase, where he concentrated his remote viewing abilities as he looked at the items in the room. Messing visualized a scene with a sloping riverbank, a small church, and a bridge across the river. There was a black item under the bridge. It was the briefcase.

Messing spoke with local geography experts, giving them the description in his mind, and they recognized two such locations in the vicinity of Moscow. Two trucks full of armed soldiers were dispatched, and a few hours later the briefcase with its precious contents was placed in front of the Soviet officials.

Messing begged Soviet scientists to study him and provide explanations for his unique abilities. But for the most part such scientists were closed-minded people, terrified of the official Communist party line, and they ignored his pleas. Some tests were carried out in the Institute of Psychiatry of the Academy of Medical Sciences, USSR. But the scientists there preferred not to discuss issues that could not be described by the ideomotor actions. The opportunity to study a new phenomenon was lost.

Wolf Messing believed in the existence of a special "field" responsible for telepathic abilities. He felt it should be discovered and researched, and that it could provide wonderful possibilities, just as the electromagnetic field did. He was also fascinated by hypnosis, and recalled that in his younger days in Poland he used hypnosis to cure mental illnesses in extreme cases.

On at least one occasion, Messing was able to predict a man's fate by looking at his photograph. He was able to foretell the future (when he was forced to by circumstances) with accuracy. Messing wrote that foresight or clairvoyance does exist. We cannot explain such phenomena because we have yet to clearly understand the essence of time, its connection to space, and the interconnectedness between past, present, and future.

The legendary artist and famous telepath worked until 1974. By then he was fluent in Russian, Polish, Hebrew and German languages. The KGB allegedly confiscated his personal diaries and notes immediately after his death. The documents remain classified.

Wolf Messing passed away in 1975, and was buried next to his wife at the Vostryakovsky cemetery of Moscow.

Chapter 15

Mystery of the Deadly Russian Ball Lightning

We know very little about the nature of ball lightning. We do not know if it is made of plasma; whether its origin is terrestrial; whether it is associated with high voltage power lines; whether it is anti-matter, an electrical discharge, a self-closed longitudinal electromagnetic wave, a nuclear reaction.... There is no explanation. We do know about the devastating effects it has had on those who have been attacked by it.

The Soviet Chronicles

Very few people in the West know of a deadly incident that took place in the Soviet Union in August 1978. A group of Soviet mountain climbers had climbed to the altitude of twelve thousand feet in the Caucasus Mountains. During the dead of night on August 17, a brightly luminescent object en-

tered their tent as they were sleeping. Viktor Kavunenko, one of the climbers, later recalled that he awoke because he felt a presence in the tent. He looked up to see a bright yellow ball.

The object then entered Oleg Korovin's sleeping bag, causing Korovin to scream in sharp pain. The ball sprung out and continued its flight over the sleeping bags, entering one after another. When it reached Kavunenko's sleeping bag, the climber felt intolerable pain, as if touched by a welding gun. He fainted.

When Kavunenko regained his senses, the strange ball was still inside the tent, attacking the mountain climbers. It was definitely following a trajectory of some kind. The men screamed from excruciating pain, but to no avail.

When the deadly mysterious object finally vanished, Oleg Korovin was dead. The others suffered various injuries. A helicopter brought them to a hospital; the doctors there concluded that the climbers' wounds were of a more serious nature than regular burns. The doctors had never seen anything similar. The results of their medical examination were mind-boggling.

The ball lightning was explained away as a natural phenomenon caused by anomalies of the atmosphere, and as such, devoid of any intellect. Yet its actions and seemingly aggressive conduct might have indicated something to the contrary. What did the doctors think of the chemical processes involved in the incident?

The muscular tissue of the Soviet mountain climbers was burned to the bones. Could this indicate a connection to spontaneous human combustion?

The ball lightning did not touch a single metal object, injuring only people. Oleg Korovin's sleeping bag was placed on a rubber mattress, insulating it from the ground.

The Caucasus incident was reported in the Soviet Weekly on February 11, 1984, and in several other Russian publications after 1991.

Usually ball lightning appears as a glowing, hovering ball of light that moves slowly near the ground before disappearing or exploding. Ball lightning is known to travel long distances. Metal in the high-energy balls will react with any water-containing substance, including flesh. When human beings touch ball lightning they can be severely burned or killed. Ball lightning carries extremely high levels of energy...but what kind of energy? What is its power supply?

There have been around 10,000 sightings of the mysterious phenomenon over the past few decades in the Soviet Union, and later Russia. One of the most interesting sightings was of an 80-centimeter glowing blob that bounced on a Russian teacher's head more than twenty times before vanishing.

In January 1984, the Soviet TASS news agency reported a case in which ball lightning entered a Soviet airline flying out of the Black Sea city of Sochi. At an altitude of 3,600 feet, a fireball about four inches in diameter appeared on the fuselage in front of the crew's cockpit. It disappeared with a raucous

noise, but reemerged several seconds later in the passenger's lounge, after passing in an eerie way through the airtight metal wall. The fireball slowly flew about the heads of the amazed passengers. In the tail section of the airliner it divided into two glowing crescents, which then joined together again and left the plane almost noiselessly.

Upon landing back at Sochi, holes were discovered in the fuselage of the Ilyushin-18 aircraft, fore and aft.

Vladimir L. Bychkov of the Russian Academy of Science's Institute for High Temperatures in Moscow put forth the proposition that ball lightning consists of a loose, porous aggregate of particles. In his theory, the heat and light come mainly from electric effects, but not oxidation. Lightning can transform many organic materials in the environment (not just metal residues from the soil) into airborne polymer threads. Once that happens, the threads can twist up into an elastic ball. Such a ball can hold electric charges in place and permit huge buildups of energy on the ball's surface, but the materials in the "twist" must be electrical insulators. The energy is stored in well separated patches (a mosaic, really) of positive and negative charges.

The newly formed ball can yield heat and light when high voltages begin breaking down gases near the surface. This process could create the orange or blue coronas that some observers have sighted.

According to an article in the June 21, 2001, issue of the Russian newspaper *Pravda*, there are many legends in Russia connected with ball lightning. The phenomenon is supposed to appear near electricity transmission lines and follows every moving object. It is believed, therefore, that one should stop moving at once when it appears. Some tales describe ball lightning drifting through windows into apartments, where fires then appear. Sometimes it even penetrates houses without breaking windowpanes.

Ball lightning still remains baffling to scientists all over the world. A fascinating report shows that people in the seventeenth century were baffled, too.

Robozero: The Ball of Fire

The Robozero sighting is the most famous UFO case in the history of ancient Russia. Yuri Roszius and other Russian researchers of paranormal phenomena have studied it extensively. The details of this amazing and enigmatic event were found within a collection of historical records published in 1842, among which was a seventeenth-century document signed by Ivan Rzhevsky, a laborer, in which he bore witness to a remarkable event.

According to Rzhevsky's testimony, on August 15, 1663, between 10:00 a.m. and noon, a great noise resounded over Robozero Lake (located in the Vologda Region, about eighty miles southwest of Belozersk). From the north, out of a clear sky, appeared a huge, flaming sphere at least 130 feet in diameter. Two beams of flame projected about twenty sazhens (140 feet) from the front of the object. From its sides poured bluish smoke. This huge ball of fire, comparable to a modern fifteen -story building, hovered over the lake. The phenomenon was observed by a multitude of people who had gathered for Mass at the parish church on the lake shore.

The noise occurred just as the thanksgiving singing had begun. Terrified by this noise, the people emerged from the church, but upon seeing the "frightful sight" they returned and "prayed to the Lord and the Virgin Mary with tears and weeping." Shortly afterwards "the great flame and the two smaller ones vanished," but it reappeared on two or three more occasions, moving in a westward direction (seemingly becoming brighter each time) before finally dimming and disappearing from view a full hour and a half later.

Peasants were sailing in a boat on the lake at the time, but the scorching heat forced them to the bank. They saw that light from the unknown object had penetrated the water and reached the bottom of the lake "about four sazhens down" (twenty-eight feet). They saw "fish fleeing from the flame toward the shore."

Another eyewitness, a peasant by the name of Levko Fedorov, corroborated Rzhevsky's story, and he also received written confirmation from the local priests that "such a token was observed on that date." Only then did Rzhevsky report the occurrence to his superiors. Despite providing a detailed description of the phenomenon, Rzhevsky does not offer any subjective interpretation of it.

Others have tried to interpret the Robozero phenomenon. Russian astronomer D. Svyatski, in his book Astronomical Phenomena in Russian Chronicles, claims that the eyewitnesses saw pieces of a meteorite that flew apart after an explosion, but this does not account for the sighting of the people in the boat approaching a hovering body. Others have tried to explain it as ball lightning, but there was no storm or rain that day. The lifespan of lightning is short, and its diameter is no more than three feet; certainly not 130 feet.

Yuri Roszius analyzed Rzhevsky's report and came up with a fresh interpretation of the sighting. His detailed analysis included the study of one interesting episode related by eyewitnesses. The document notes a change in the outer appearance of the object: an increase in its brightness when it came into view for the third time. For some reason this change preceded the start of the object's progressive movement westward. In modern times, such an increase in brightness could be attributed to the firing-up of cruise engines (an increase in its thrust). Is it by chance that the object's brightness increased before its departure?

Mankind did not possess such advanced technology then, but it is possible that the population of Robozero was being observed by an alien civilization. To this day, no known scientific theory has explained the phenomenon.

Chapter 16

Russian Armed Forces and Astrology

In 2003, Russian academicians Aleksandrov, Ginzburg, Kruglyakov, and Fortov launched an attack in the form of a letter on the pages of the famous *Izvestiya* newspaper (October 28, 2003). The target of their attack was "pseudoscience," or rather its dominance in the Russian Army. They were extremely upset by the fact that the Cultural Center of the Armed Forces of the Russian Federation houses an entity called Center of Scientific Astrology. This fact irks them, and runs, claim the academicians, contrary to common sense. Astrology has nothing to do with science, and from Cicero to our times great thinkers have discredited astrology. As an example to prove their point, the academicians recalled the case of a high-ranking Russian military official who had predicted five or so years earlier that a thermonuclear war was to start in the summer of 1999. Also, a certain Captain of First Rank by the name of A. Buzinov, well known to the Russian media, a military clairvoyant, has been known to frequent the Ministry of Defense and the General Staff of the Russian Armed Forces.

Who Is Captain Buzinov?

Buzinov is a fascinating personality in modern Russia. We should not limit our introduction of him to views of Russian academicians who completely reject astrology.

In December 1997, Russian naval captain Alexander Buzinov told a Moscow TV interviewer that he was employed as an astrologer for the military, examining "planetary rhythms" effects on the Earth's surface." Such rhythms, he claimed, led him to successfully predict three personnel firings last year, along with terrorist acts in the Caucasus, a Siberian transport plane crash, and several of Boris Yeltsin's medical conditions.

The same year, the Russian Navy was anxiously trying to torpedo a report by *Pravda* in St. Petersburg that suggested that a department in the Ministry of Defense received regular predictions from an astrology team. Buzinov, who, the paper said, headed the astrology unit, claimed his work was aimed at providing predictions rather than trying to avert catastrophe.

Alexander Buzinov.

A Russian Navy spokesperson assured the media that the captain's duties had nothing to do with astrology, but he did admit that astrology was Buzinov's hobby.

In 1998, Buzinov boasted to a British newspaper that Russian military astrologers were bucking the trend of decline in the Russian military establishment. He claimed that Russian astrologers were superior to their American and Japanese counterparts and insisted that they were able to predict the time and place of disasters, assassinations, and military incidents with great accuracy.

In January 2002, in an interview with *Pravda*, Buzinov revealed a few details about himself.

Buzinov had been the supervisor of the laboratory for space and astrological forecasts of the Russian Defense Ministry. And he did make a series of correct predictions: the sinking of the Estonia ferryboat, the acts of terrorism in the town of Budyonovsk, the scandal with the Russian NTV television network, Yeltsin's early resignation, and the events of September 11, 2001, in the United States. Buzinov also predicted several natural disasters, man-caused catastrophes, breakdowns, and other states of emergency.

Buzinov graduated from a naval electronics college, and served his country in the Soviet northern territories and later in Angola. There, a fellow officer introduced him to astrology. Coming back to the disintegrating Soviet Union, Buzinov enrolled in an academy of astrology (there were many "academies" like that in the heady perestroika days). After he became supervisor of the Defense Ministry's astrology lab, Buzinov accurately predicted the explosion of warehouses in Vladivostok, the collision of submarines, and the withdrawal of Russian troops from Yemen. He also predicted that Putin would become the president of Russia. Buzinov underwent many tests and scientific probes. Later he worked in the Scientific Research Institute of the Russian Air Force and made many more forecasts.

Buzinov's rate of accurate predictions is impressive. How is he able to see the future? His explanation is as follows: the rhythm of a human life is determined by the interactions of the space and physical factors of his birth with the solar activity, solar and lunar cycles, and the movement of the planets. At the same time, two people born in one and the same place can have totally different lives because they have different parents. That is why Buzinov and his colleagues use the so-called rhythm-driving factors in their forecasts. They forecast a complex of the influences on a human being, the technological influence, the influence of the region on the possibility of the worst-case situations to happen. His theory in Russian is known as *lokal'niy geofizicheskiy rezonans,* or LGR. According to his fierce opponents, the above-mentioned academicians, Buzinov and A. Sinyakov, his scientist-colleague, have a number of supporters among Russia's top governmental officials. But to the academicians, the LGR is on par with astrology; i.e., a pseudoscience.

The Russian Ministry of Nuclear Power had used Buzinov's services; Buzinov and colleagues were studying the situation at all Russian nuclear power plants, per the Ministry's request, and warned them about a possible danger at one of those nuclear plants. The Ministry took adequate security measures.

As for his predictions for the future of the world at the time of the interview (January 4, 2002), Buzinov said that the second half of the year 2003 and the year 2008 may be the most difficult times in the future.

The academicians listed a number of Buzinov's failed predictions. They are upset by the fact that the captain has been called upon to help the Prosecutor General solve criminal cases. They hasten to add that according to a source there he failed but provide no details.

Unit 10003

What interested me the most in the letter published in *Izvestiya* was the following information revealed by the academicians. Lately they have noticed a "sad" trend: Russian laws enforcement ministries have employed astrologers, sorcerers, and magical practitioners, psychics, and "scientists" who have nothing to do with science. The Ministry of Defense of the Russian Federation is in the forefront of this trend. It still has the military unit 10003. The "science" that blossoms in this military unit can exist only due to the regime of mindless secrecy, according to the academicians.

Russia is using the paranormal to beef up its security and defense. Perhaps Captain Buzinov is more effective than his critics show him to be. And perhaps someday soon we will learn about the secret unit 10003.

Chapter 17

Russian Precognition Cases

Precognition is the direct knowledge or perception of the future, obtained through extrasensory means. It is a psychic knowledge of something in advance of its occurrence.

Lomonosov

Mikhail Vasilyevich Lomonosov (1711–1765) was a Russian writer, chemist, and astronomer, who made important contributions to both literature and science. Among his many accomplishments, Lomonosov published the first history of Russia in 1760 and was the first to observe the atmosphere of Venus during a solar transit.

In 1822, *Russkiy Arkhiv*, a Russian magazine, published the memoirs of academician Yakov Shtelin, who was Lomonosov's friend. Shtelin revealed a fascinating episode of the scientist's life.

On his way by sea from Arkhangelsk to St. Petersburg, Lomonosov had a strange dream. He saw his father shipwrecked and lying dead on a small island in the White Sea. The isle had no name, but Lomonosov knew it well, for he and his father had once been driven there by a storm.

As soon as he arrived in St. Petersburg, Lomonosov sought out some merchants from his home region, asking for news of his father. He learned that his father had embarked on a fishing trip the previous autumn and had never returned.

Lomonosov was shocked by the news, and by his own prophetic dream. Though he wanted to travel home to give his father a proper burial, his studies in St. Petersburg prevented him from leaving. He sent a letter with the merchants to his brother, beseeching him to find their father's body immediately and sending instructions on how to find the island on which he believed it was located.

That very summer Lomonosov's request was executed: a group of Russian fishermen landed on the deserted isle, found the remains of his father, and buried them. This news brought relief to the scientist, who had been despondent ever since his visionary dream.

The Officer's Wife

Russian painter V. Krashenninikov, in his youth, had a close friend whose last name was Nechiporenko. Nechiporenko once shared a mysterious family legend with Krashenninikov.

Nechiporenko's aunt had married a young Russian military officer on the eve of the Russo-Japanese war. When the war broke out, the officer was ordered to leave for the Far East. The young couple despaired, but the officer obeyed his duty. He sent his young wife to his parents' estate and left for Manchuria. She received his letters frequently at first, but then they stopped coming. The officer's family became quite worried.

The officer's wife often sought refuge in the grand ballroom of the ancient Russian house. Once she lay there on a sofa, lost in her thoughts, looking at a mirror that hung on the wall between two windows. Eventually, her eyelids closed, although she kept staring at the mirror in her mental vision.

She experienced a strange, half-conscious state. Her attention was attracted by visions that seemed to arise from the depth of the mirror. She saw hills overgrown with trees and covered with snow.

Suddenly she observed motion in the snow: someone clad in a white camouflage cloak was slowly moving on all fours. She looked deeper and recognized her husband and his orderly. They crawled in the snow, glancing around. Then she observed two other people who also moved surreptitiously, but much quicker than the Russians. They were Japanese, and they were holding knives in their teeth as they crawled. One of them approached her husband and raised his knife over him. The terrified young woman opened her eyes, and not fully realizing what she was doing, grabbed the first object she found at the table and threw it at the Japanese.

The loud sound of breaking glass attracted attention; people ran into the ballroom and found the young woman lying unconscious on the floor. When she came to her senses the next day, the young woman told her story and her father-in-law wrote it down in great detail.

Several weeks later the officer arrived at his parents' estate quite unexpectedly. He had been given a short leave in connection with a mysterious and quite inexplicable incident. He and his orderly were sent to do reconnaissance. They donned special white camouflage cloaks and crawled behind the enemy lines. Suddenly they heard a woman's scream and sounds of broken glass. Jumping to their feet they saw two Japanese men with knives in their hands. Both were dead, although their bodies were still warm.

The officer's father told him that they already knew about the incident, because his young wife had seen it in her dream. Across thousands of miles, she had saved the lives of her husband and his orderly.

Chapter 18

Soviet Mind Control Experiments

It is time to tell the world about Soviet psychic warfare. Although this is only a partial history of Soviet efforts to research and develop *psi-oruzhiye* (psychic weapons), it is the most complete account ever published in the West.

The Odessa Research

In 1991, an article entitled "Once More About Psychic Weapons" was published in the *Ugolog Ukraini* newspaper (Issue 3, 1991) by A. V. Kalinets-Bryukhanov (K.B.), president of the All-Union Scientific Research Association for the Study of Psychophysical Problems of Nature.

Ivan Demyanovich Buryak, the newspaper's editor and my acquaintance, forwarded the article to me at the Russian Ufology Research Center.

K.B. stated that the first (and only) experimental model of a device to program the human intellect and psyche had been accepted by Soviet authorities back in 1965. It was to be improved using K.B.'s design for a system of "remote operational influence." However, to cover up the device's existence, the Soviets continued experiments to screen it. False experiments were needed because B. I. Askakov, Ph.D. (Science of Economics), had some ambitious plans, so some information about the device was leaked abroad.

As a result, "*Extrasensy? Marsh V Stroy!* (Psychics? Get Back In Line)" appeared in *Moskovskaya Pravda* (May 3, 1983). No names were mentioned.

Psychic Weapons Exist

K.B. stated that the "much-buzzed about psychic weapons" do exist. In April 1983 he participated in the development of one of the most classified projects of the Soviet State Committee for Science and Technologies. The work was subsidized by a departmental research laboratory of the Soviet military-industrial complex. This took place shortly before Boris Ivanovich Askakov, then professor at the Moscow Institute of National Economy, had partially blown the cover off the secret research, allegedly dubbing it "microleptonnic weapons."

K.B. was employed as a researcher at the V.P. Filatov Institute of Eye Diseases and Tissue Therapy in the city of Odessa, where he was involved in equally classified research into the effects of electromagnetic pulse fields. He studied various effects of the exertion of force upon cellular structures and subcellular formations.

Simultaneously, more sinister research was taking place at Odessa Mechnikov Soviet State University. It involved the development of an electronic device to direct remote influence upon the biological environment, using microwave radiation, with subsequent corrections of biophysical parameters of living organisms.

Due to an agreement between the two institutes, K.B. worked at the juncture of the two scientific research projects. So he was clearly the choice to help develop a new type of weapon system, which was designated to be the future weapon of choice for all branches of the Soviet armed forces.

Incognito Research

All of the research was done secretly in a small basement beneath the old botanical gardens of Odessa State University, the site of the Bioelectronics Scientific Research Department (part of the physics department).

Special couriers arrived from Moscow for research reports, of which there was always only one copy. The scientists were then to forget about the contents of the reports. Even K.B.'s immediate superiors knew nothing about his secret research work.

The head of the Filatov Institute Ultrasound Lab, who was responsible for the Communist Party organizational work at the Institute, was not deemed trustworthy enough to know about the secret research. Because the primary research topic of the institute was the human eye, the issue of whether the secret research was proper was easily resolved.

At the scientists' disposal were spectrophotometers, electronic microscopes, a chemistry lab, nuclear molecular resonants, and a menagerie of animals for experiments.

Tests on animal brains demonstrated that when cellular transformation resulted from fields of especially destructive force, manifestations of paranormal abilities like clairvoyance became possible. When the animals were treated with these fields, they could literally see through opaque barriers.

Death Sentence Prisoners Experimented On

It was a short-term phenomenon that, due to the uncontrolled disintegration of brain tissue, resulted in physical death of the animal. K.B. later found that similar experiments had been conducted on prisoners sentenced to death. The results were the same.

Later, using the experimental data, the researchers located phrenological zones of the skull responsible for motivating various actions. The topography of these zones was recorded in special tables. These experiments helped Soviet scientists find the most effective electromagnetic-pulse-field operating conditions to reproduce cerebral tissue that would create the planned personality characteristic. For example:

Grigory V. was a draftee in the Soviet Army assigned to serve in Afghanistan. His health was quite good. After his assignment with the *spetznaz* forces, Grigory became indecisive. He became obsessed with the feeling of near death. He believed that he was not "sufficiently strong spiritually" to enforce his "international duty" (as the Soviets described their occupation of Afghanistan).

So he and a group of other draftees who, like him, had their doubts about service in Afghanistan were sent to Odessa to undergo the treatment and develop their will power and sense of duty. Magnetic emitters were placed on his superciliary arches, the parietal area, the cranial arch, and the cervical vertebrae area. Grigory was treated only once.

Later that year, Grigory took part in a dangerous military mission. His *spetznaz* unit was withdrawing from a *kishlak*, an Afghan village. *Dooshmany* (guerrillas) surrounded the *kishlak*. During a fierce gun battle, Grigory protected the commanding officer with his body. For his valor, the fallen soldier was awarded the highest Soviet military honor, the star of Hero of the Soviet Union.

K.B. ended his article strangely. Having observed the brain as a receiving and transmitting device, the researchers had discovered certain wavelengths. Using them, it is possible to influence various sections of the brain directly, reproduce cerebral tissue, and then provoke unusual changes in the qualities of individual psyches. Then one can program anything into the brains of experimental subjects.

On July 4, 1991, a month before the August 1991 coup in the Soviet Union, a curious document known as *Resolution 58 of the Committee for Science and Technologies of the Supreme Soviet of the USSR* came from the Kremlin. The resolution condemned the "depraved practice" of financing pseudoscientific research with state funds.

The research in question was of "nontraditional technologies" and had been conducted in the scientific research centers of the Academy of Sciences of the USSR, the Academies of Sciences of several Soviet republics, and a number of state ministries and departments. Particularly, it was research into the so-called spinor (torsionnic) or microleptonnic fields.

The research was tied to the creation of an unusual organization in the Soviet State Committee for Science and Technologies. It became known as the Center for Non-traditional Technologies (CNT); its former director was A. E. Akimov.

The research work had been going on, according to Akimov, for over thirty years. In the last ten years prior to 1991, there had been practical technological applications of the results. The research was based on assertions that there had been an unprecedented discovery in the science of physics. It had to do with a new class of physical fields and particles, and the influence exerted by such fields upon biological objects, inorganic nature, instruments, and equipment.

The resolution stated that Soviet science officialdom knew nothing of such discoveries, either through open publications or closed channels, and that there had been only one private publication of the subject which was by then refuted. The information presented by CNT'S officials, whether through reports, presentations, or publications, essentially contradicted conceptions established by modern science.

Aside from the quasi-scientific terminology used in such reports, the information was unsubstantiated, illogical, and scientifically unfounded. The CNT itself was created without the necessary expertise.

Pseudo-science Blossoms

Later, the research was legitimized by support given it by the State Committee. Because of such support, the USSR Ministry of Defense and other state agencies had enough grounds to create a special research center, VENT. Akimov became its general director. Millions of rubles were spent as the projects of VENT received state funding. Akimov states that the USSR Ministry of Defense alone had spent twenty-three million rubles, an impressive amount. According to him, total funding for VENTfrom the USSR Military-Industrial Commission of the Cabinet of Ministers and the KGB was five hundred million rubles.

The resolution states that the investigative committee took into consideration the conclusions of the Department of General Physics and Astronomy of the Academy of Sciences, USSR. These conclusions characterized the research work in the areas of spinor and microleptonnic fields and their applications as a recurrence of anti-scientific activity.

The committee blamed the irresponsible approach taken by state agencies toward scientific expertise for the waste of state funds allocated for "anti-scientific activities." This was a clear abuse of the secrecy regime in Soviet academic institutions. The latter, as well as some colleges, had been involved in the whole mess.

The circulation of unclear information about similar research efforts abroad assisted the "blossoming of pseudo-science," but no convincing confirmation ever existed. The committee finally requested several things:

1. Expert reports before funds would be allocated.

2. Control over completed or planned work in non-traditional fields.

3. Reports of the sums spent, and the sources for the financing used for microleptonnic and other projects, were mildly requested from the KGB, the military, and the nuclear R&D establishment.

One month later, the Soviet Union was shaken to its foundations and began to fall apart. Yet, on September 9, 1991, the *Komsomolskaya Pravda* newspaper published an unusual article. Its author, Mr. Volkov, revealed what the CNT had actually researched. His source was a report from the CNT, *Main Directions of Research.*

The CNT was involved in the study of remote medical and biological influences on the armed forces and people exposed to torsionnic radiation; remote psychophysical influence on members of the armed forces and others from the same radiation; and, finally, defense to exposure from torsionnic radiation.

In the fall of 1991, Emil Fedorovich Bachurin in the Soviet city of Perm wrote a two-part article in issues 34 and 35 of *Molodaya Gvardia* magazine. He described the kinds of weapons that fall under the heading of "psychotronic." Bachurin calls his information "materials about the secret system of MOB-resources." The weapons are dreadful. A human being becomes a silent cog in a hellish machine of all-devouring fear. An individual's brain can be suppressed, his activities curtailed, and his individual will subjected to any wish of the operator.

Weapons from Nazi Germany

Bachurin repeats an account of experiments to create psi-weapons allegedly conducted by the infamous Dr. Josef Mengele in the Dachau concentration camp. He is not the only one to mention the Nazi research.

In July 1993, Alexander Ryskin, a Russian journalist, published an article in Los Angeles (*Almanac Panorama*) in which he claims that the Nazis were able to use such technology to hinder the Soviet offensive in Berlin in May of 1945.

The Soviets captured the results of Nazi research and brought them to the Soviet Union, but more proof, documentation, or something tangible to substantiate the rumors is necessary. Certainly, Nazi Germany's evil, inhuman regime was capable of carrying out such research. But wouldn't Stalin proceed with his own psi-weapons research, having obtained the fruits of Adolf Hitler's labor?

Yet Ryskin's source informed him that no serious research took place after WW II in the USSR until 1979. But Akimov of the CNT indicates that the research started in the early 1960s. This is confirmed by K.B.; 1965 is specifically mentioned.

Bachurin claims that several centers for the development of parapsychological weapons had operated in Canada, and that one still does. He also says that similar research took place under Lavrenty Beria, chief of the USSR secret police, and that his successors continued that research. Finally, it was

Un Andropov, head of the KGB, who issued personal orders to his subordinates that the Canadian research was to be surpassed.

Ryskin claims that no serious research took place until a group of underground Soviet scientists who conducted their own research was captured by the KGB in 1979. The same source informed Ryskin that the first psi-generators were tested in 1983 on a group of Soviet soldiers at a firing range near Moscow. Taking into account K.B.'s version, 1983 begins to take on a sinister glow.

Bachurin's source for the Andropov episode is the former KGB General Kalugin, who revealed the information at Krasnodar in August of 1990. Bachurin lists several types of *psi-oruzhiye*:

The first, most effective, well-known, destructive type tortures the victim and then kills him. It is based on infrasonic radiation at seven Hertz. The human brain and peripheral nervous system cannot withstand such directed radiation. It is easy to produce such a weapon, but it will kill all humans in its operational area, including the operator. The secret of putting it to proper use is finding the right screening emitter; none had been developed as of fall 1991.

Application of directed, high-power microwave and ultrasound radiation is the principle behind the second type of psi-weapons. Although these are two separate concepts, each one affects the nervous system equally effectively: humans lose sleep. Insomnia wrecks a human being, and such weapons can be made portable.

The third type of *psi-oruzhiye* involves several systems: chronal emitters, chronal guns, pyramid sets, and some cavity structures. The destructive effect here is achieved by creation of chronal beams, consisting of tiny particles—chronos, or time carriers. Such beams are all penetrating, and their velocity allows the beams to disperse in space instantaneously.

After a volley from a chronal gun, the human aura is torn to pieces, and the victim's bioenergy defense is gone. Should the energy circle (halo or nimbus) around an individual's head be hit, the mental abilities of the targeted person will be affected. Such weapons do not kill, but they maim the psyche. Prolonged exposure to bullets from such weapon systems can affect the urinary system, sexual organs, the cranial brain, and the spinal cord. Leukemia and malignant brain tumors are the results.

The fourth type, and by far the most dangerous for human targets (but safe for the operator) is the psi-generator. It is also known as a psi-amplifier, and psi-data unit. And generators they truly are. What is being generated is electromagnetic radiation that conforms to brain frequencies.

Such radiation, when directed at the target, can be used to suggest and transmit anything, any feeling—love, hate, euphoria, anger, anguish, and suicidal thoughts. The psi-generators can be used for remote transmission.

Creators of such generators designed defenses to shield the operator's brain. If hit directly, the victim loses his will power, and should the person be excited or think intensely about something at the time of the attack, the victims suffer cerebral thrombosis.

Bachurin concludes by demanding complete *glastnost* about any development of such weapons. He is worried because such psi-generators are in serial production, but not all of them are controlled by the state—some are homemade.

Espionage

The July 1993 issue of *Chetvertoye Izmereniye Y Nb*, published in the Russian city of Yaroslavi, contained an article written by V. Scheglov, a research associate.

Based on information in his possession, he claims that there is plenty of proof to confirm the use of modern psychic weapons against civilian populations.

There is hope, Scheglov continues, that the "telepathic counterintelligence services of Russia and the United States" will soon cease to exist. He mentions that there is preparatory work under way inside the former Soviet counterintelligence to achieve that purpose.

The work was to be finished by June 20, 1993. Scheglov laments that so-called declassification is proceeding at a very slow pace. And he again mentions indisputable evidence that it is due to the fault of the telepathic counterintelligence departments of the KGB and the CIA, that terrestrial civilization has not been able to establish official contacts with alien intelligence.

The Ministry of Security of the Russian Federation, the CIA, and special services of other countries possess testimonies convincing enough to conclude that there is the presence of a "detachment of observers" from other worlds in near-Earth orbit. The security agencies of leading countries of our planet know well that the reconnaissance mission of ET civilizations has one centralized command body responsible for coordination, planning, and enforcement of large-scale activities to study and observe Earth.

Several conferences took place in the USSR. In 1988 and 1990, there were two scientific seminars in the Siberian city of Tomsk. Because new technologies and phenomena were discussed, numerous representatives of the KGB, the Ministry of Defense, and the Ministry of the Interior Affairs were actively collecting information on new ideas, trends, and inventions. Some scientists, along with their inventions, were bought, either openly or clandestinely. Technologies that could be used for the development of psi-weapons were discussed.

Another conference took place in 1990, the "Bioenergoinform.90." There were three hundred people present, half of them some of the most powerful psychics of the former USSR. They had conducted experiments with directed radiation and insomnia as a side effect of microwave radiation.

In 1989 an international symposium dedicated to the issues of psychotronics took place in Moscow. One topic discussed was the issue of studying such phenomena as clairvoyance, telepathy, telekinesis, prognostication, and "vision of the past." All of the issues had to do with parapsychology. Examples were presented to prove the existence of such phenomena; test results were discussed; hypotheses proffered.

Sources Used

All information and dates used are based on documented sources. The Soviet scientific vernacular vocabulary used in this article is translated directly from Russian.

Among the dictionaries used for the translation work, there was a very curious one: the *English-Russian Dictionary of Antimissile & Anti-satellite Defense,* Moscow, 1989, published by Military Publishing House.

Further Revelations

After the publication of an article entitled "Soviet Psychic Warfare" in the February 1994 issue of FATE magazine, I collected more information about the development of psychological weapons (*psi-oruzhiye*) in the former Soviet Union. I have also received a well-researched and most informative article by Barbara Opall, published in the January 1993 issue of *Defense News* (Washington, D.C.). The headline reads, "U.S. Explores Russian Mind-Control Technology." Opall's article concerned the Russian military's willingness to share its mind control technology with American military and scientists.

It is my conclusion that Russia has not abandoned the research and development (R&D) on *psioruzhiye*, and perhaps has even shared some of it with the U.S. This article covers some of the information I have received from my Russian sources.

The September 1992 issue of *Tekhnika Molodezhi* magazine contains a most curious article. Its author, Stanislav Zigunenko, an engineer, mentions those KGB officers who knew about the psychotronic weapons programs and Soviet "truth serums." One of them is ex-KGB Col. Yaroslav Karpovich. In an interview on the *Freedom* radio program, Karpovich discussed activities of the KGB directorates that "handled" the "extrasensy" (psychics), as well as the devices that were built based on parapsychological technologies.

It is interesting to note that just several years prior to that period (late 1980s), the KGB bosses had considered the "extrasensy" to be nothing but psychos and nuts, the actual achievements of applied parapsychology as well as procurement of factual information about similar programs being developed and used by foreign intelligence services had caused the KGB decision-makers to change. It is clear that Zigunenko did not know of the "Odessa Research"—a program where Russian soldiers who refused to serve in Afghanistan were forcibly experimented on with "psi generators"—or other, earlier Soviet *psior-uzhiye* developments. The Soviets, I believe—and Opall's article seems to confirm—were ahead of their Western counterparts.

In an article published in *Stolitsa* magazine (Russia, 1992), another former KGB officer, Valentin Korolyov, mentions the sinister ZOMBIE program. The program allegedly used agents— "zombies"—that is, people whose subconscious minds had been pumped with espionage assignments and "cover legends" ; the actual procedure or "pumping" is an elaborate form of hypnosis. According to Karpovich, only a very skilful hypnotist, one proficient in all sixteen levels of hypnosis, can rework the zombie's mind.

However, back in November 1991, the scientific-technical directorate of the KGB had publicly responded to similar allegations in the *Konsomolskya Pravda* newspaper: no similar devices for influencing the human psyche have ever been developed by KGB. But in the Soviet *List of Information Authorized for Publication* (by any media entities) as of 1990, the information that is "unauthorized" (actually, the word *zapreshennikh* should be translated as "banned," "forbidden") includes any data "about technical means (generators, emitters) for influencing human behavioral functions (creation of biorobots)..." Here is what else was banned in 1990: data about Soviet military personnel becoming ill after handling the microwave-emitting devices; scientific R&D in the area of creation and use of microwave-generators by military, as well as the effects of radiation from such devices on various military objects and people.

In 1992, Russian newspapers carried reports about a lecture delivered by two arcane inventors. One of them refused to reveal his name, the other one is named I. Kachalin. The lecture-presentation was titled "Influence on biological objects by modulated electric and electromagnetic pulses." The lecture was presented at the bioelectronics lab of the Institute of Radioelectronics of the Academy of Sciences, USSR. Kachalin, not revealing too many details, had reported that the lecture mentioned means of remote artificial sleep imposition through the use of radio waves.

Back in 1973, in one of the Novosibirsk (Siberia) military units, a radio device dubbed RADIOSON (Radiosleep) had been tested (guess who it was tested on?). The device contained a microwave generator. The report about all experiments conducted was signed by academician Y. B. Kobzarev; the military angle was provided by Marshal of Aviation E. Savitsky. However, the projects were never completed, according to the inventors of the sinister RADIOSON device. Zigunenko offers two explanations: either similar projects had been conducted elsewhere (parallel R&D, at a more secret level, that resulted in the creation of a psychotronic generator), or the results that the Novosibirsk people sought were not achieved.

The human brain is too fragile for our modern technology to force it to become a "zombie," or whatever else the KGB inheritors want it to become…or is it? My research of the Odessa R&D (the Kalinets-Bryukhanov testimony), and other secret projects, seems to contradict the notion that the human brain is too fragile. Had the Soviets conducted experiments on Aldrich Ames's mind, to help that alleged traitor be able to successfully deceive his bosses? Or were they using him as bait, after they "pumped" his psyche to flaunt his ill-gotten wealth, in order to protect another, much more important mole? I suspect they were—unless the man was really stupid and greedy, and I doubt it.

A related article appeared in 1994 in *Defense Electronics* magazine. In it, writer Mark Tapscott quotes an anonymous source who reportedly participated in FBI meetings with Dr. Igor Smimov of the Moscow Medical Academy, along with assorted U.S. defense and intelligence officials. At those briefings, the FBI heard about a Russian acoustic mind control device, which they would consider using on David Koresh, the Branch Davidian leader killed with seventy of his followers in a fiery confrontation at the group's compound in Waco, Texas.

The device, its Russian developers said, was capable of implanting thoughts in a person's mind. Because the Russians couldn't promise "zero risk" with the use of the device, and because a more advanced model would have had to have been quickly shipped to the U.S. for use on Koresh, the FBI decided against the plan.

A recently published book sent to me from Moscow deals with the subject of Soviet and Russian psychotronic warfare. A cornucopia of useful information, it is a fascinating book, full of details previously unavailable in the West. However, the Russian authors did not have information about the sinister Odessa research which had been made available to me, reports which told of psychotronic and pulse field experiments on living organisms, including humans, and the development of a device to program the human intellect and psyche. (See my article in the February 1994 issue of FATE magazine.)

In April 1994 I received a curious publication from Moscow. Called "The Unknown World," it's a joint publication of the Russian Information Agency, Academy of Informatization (sic), and the CIS Ufological Association.

The January 1994 issue of *The Unknown World* (*Mir Nepoznannogo* in Russian) contained an article written by Vladimir Georgiyev entitled "Psychotronic Nightmare: Hysteria Gathers in the Media Around Mysterious Weapons." Georgiyev could not know of my research; he was not aware of the psychotronic device (see above); he knew nothing of the Odessa experiments on human beings. And yet, it is very important to review Georgiyev's article because of the information it does contain.

The author was very much disturbed by something that the *Moskkovsky Kosomolets* newspaper featured on August 28, 1993. It was an article written by Oleg Sklyarenko and Yuri Ryazhsky; apparently it discussed the "Zombie Program."

It is rumored that the KGB had used specialized hypnosis and "psyche programming" to train its operatives. Of course, similar techniques were used on various dissidents and, quite probably, on intelligence agents/defectors to break them down. Author Georgiyev calls the article "an intricate canard."

What are his arguments? After all, such prestigious Russian magazines as *Tekhnika Molodezhi* (September 1992) had already discussed the KGB officers who knew about the psychotronic weapons research programs and Soviet "truth serums." Discussing the latest local wars, Georgiyev shows that such weapons were never used in practice, although there is no denying that some states are designing the technology and methods of psychotronic effects on human beings and equipment for military purposes.

As is known, the research in this sphere is so far purely experimental and highly classified. Are they being tested on human beings on a mass scale? It is highly improbable that any ruling structure would dare to issue such orders. Such are the author's arguments. Let us now see his further reasoning.

We already know that "some states" were none other than the Soviet Union, and the experiments conducted on those soldiers who refused to serve in Afghanistan were not purely experimental. Georgiyev was an officer aboard a submarine in the Soviet Northern Navy. He had experienced the effects electromagnetic and sound waves have on a human being and living matter. He was stunned to find out that cats brought on board by crew members for homelike comfort did not live longer than three days, and had the animals been placed in the battery or power sections of the submarine, they could not have lasted hours. The detrimental effect of microwaves on living organisms is well known.

Low-frequency waves measured in Hertz units are known to the Russian public from publications about the Bermuda Triangle. According to one hypothesis, confirmed by academician Vladimir Shulenik's research, infrasonic vacillations may affect movement coordination and mental states of ships' crew members.

As far as Georgiyev knows, some countries have designed, but never used, methods of dispersing rallies by causing pain to protestors through the use of infrasound generators installed on specially equipped vehicles. He also read a scientific paper that analyzed the depressing effect infrasonic vacillations generated by tractor engines have on testers. Thus, Georgiyev does not challenge the notion of harmful waves and effects on human beings. He just does not believe that there are devices that can produce and direct such "effects" on human beings.

But some of his own data makes that assumption inaccurate. Georgiyev tells of a Russian scientist, Alexander Okhatrin, who did study the so-called microlepton fields and designed a device for their generation. It has never been the researcher's intention to use the device as a psychotronic weapon. I thank Georgiyev for that valuable bit of information. Now we have proof, however tenuous, of yet another Soviet or Russian-made device that could be a prototype of a psychotronic weapon.

The book *Psikhotronnaya Voina* mentions another very sinister phenomenon in post-Soviet Russia: underground science working hand-in-hand with the criminal underworld. In secret underground laboratories (one of the authors claims to have visited such a lab), dangerous devices are being created by top scientists. Some of the devices are designed with the aim of changing, subjugating, and controlling the human psyche.

Back in 1991, the *Mosskovskiye Novosti* newspaper published a report about such laboratories. Since then their number has undoubtedly increased, as law and order continue to break down in Russia. Some underground laboratories specialize in the removal of vital organs from Russians who simply "disappear" from the streets of their home towns. Specially designed vehicles, often "pseudo-ambulances" or "police cars," are used to kidnap them. Some, as we have found out, specialize in the removal of one's psyche.

Chapter 19

Walking into a Minefield

Anthropoid Chimera Experiments

A "chimera"—originally the fabulous Greek mythological creature with a lion's head, a goat's body, and a serpent's tail—has come to mean any hybrid of two or more creatures.

Chimpanzees are believed by many scientists to be the closest relatives of humans. The genetic difference between the two species is estimated to be about 1.7 percent at the DNA level (less than that between horses and zebras). Recent progress in studies of DNA sequences, the fossil record, and brain functions support the idea that there is a sizeable gap separating chimpanzees and monkeys, but not chimpanzees and humans.

Many years ago, according to the recently declassified Soviet documents, a famous scientist tried to close the gap between *Homo sapiens* and Pan troglodytes.

Human-Ape Hybrids

Ilya Ivanovich Ivanov was born in 1870. In 1898, he established several zoological laboratories in Moscow, where he studied the reproductive processes of farm animals. In 1901, he established the world's first center for artificially impregnated horses. Before and after the Bolshevik revolution, Ivanov applied his practical technique to other domesticated species. Several million cattle and sheep were artificially inseminated by the mid-1930s; the Soviets needed strong animals for their monumental transformation of the economy. Ivanov also tried to preserve some endangered species using artificial insemination.

In 1927, the Russian émigré newspaper *Russkoye Vremya* published articles concerning shocking experiments in which Ivanov allegedly tried to artificially inseminate human and ape females with the other species' sperm. Few people, however, believed these reports. Many in the West at the time were supporting the "progressive" Soviet Republic.

Proof came after the fall of the Soviet Union, according to Alexander Potapov, who published his research in *Na Grani nevozhmozhnogo* newspaper (issue 335/4, 2004). A document was discovered in the state archives of the Russian Federation reporting the findings of a special commission created in 1929 to evaluate Ivanov's proposed anthropoid interspecies hybridization experiments. These experiments were considered to be of "great scientific importance," and the report indicated that they were to be continued in the Sukhumi Monkey Colony, a Soviet primate center.

The hybridization experiments (the artificial insemination of human females by anthropoid sperm) were to be conducted only with the written agreement of the female. She would accept the risk and obey the required strict isolation regime. The experiments were to be conducted with all necessary safeguards, including preclusion of natural insemination. The trials were to be conducted on as many human females as possible, but in no case, fewer than five.

Why would the luminaries of Soviet science laud Ivanov's uncanny research? According to Potapov, the Bolshevik elite wanted to destroy the belief in God, and subject nature to serve the new Soviet Man. As a former Soviet citizen myself, I can affirm that neither general ethical concerns nor Judeo-Christian beliefs would be of any interest to Soviet Marxists.

Stalin, whose bloody star was rising in the crimson world of Soviet politics, would get hybrid slaves who would be completely obedient. The GULAG and its network of concentration camps would not be a necessity for the hybrids.

Ivanov and the socialist motherland were interested in another result of crossbreeding, referred to as hybrid vigor, or heterosis. Heterosis levels tend to be higher as a result of crossbreeding, meaning that the vigor of the hybrids is greater than that of the parental lines.

I am sure that Stalin and his henchmen would have found another use for the chimeric anthropoids designed by Ivanov. Today we call it biological warfare.

Guinea

Ivanov decided that an expedition to Africa would help him achieve the necessary results. He put in a request, and received an approval from the Soviet government. He also was given a financial support in the amount of $291,912, a huge amount of money for the impoverished socialist state.

Ivanov believed that he would have no problems inseminating African women with chimpanzee sperm. But he was wrong. Local women refused to crossbreed with apes. The Russian scientist would not give up, and made an agreement with physicians in a local hospital to conduct the intramural hybridization experiments. The governor of the province did not object to the experiments on the condition that the patients would agree to it. But the women of Guinea categorically refused to be any part of the lurid experiments of the Soviet scientist.

Ivanov was arrested on December 13, 1930, and sentenced to a concentration camp for five years. The OGPU (the forerunner of the KGB) commuted his sentence to a five-year exile in Kazakhstan, and finally, Ivanov was released from prison in 1932. He died just a few months later, on March 20. But our story does not end here.

USSR

In 1974, Belgian zoologist Bernard Heuvelmans and Soviet scientist Boris F. Porchnev published a fascinating book entitled *L'homme de Néanderthal est toujours vivant.* This book contains the account of a Russian doctor who escaped from the Soviet concentration camps, and in 1952 or 1953 met a trusted friend of Heuvelmans. The doctor claimed that he was arrested because he refused to obey the orders from his superiors. He was to conduct artificial insemination of Oriental women by the sperm of male gorillas. The experiments were conducted in the medical department of the Soviet forced labor camps. The doctor claimed that a race of apemen was created. They were extremely strong and covered with fur, worked tirelessly in the salt mines, and grew larger than the humans—but they could not reproduce.

Did the Soviets create an apeman in their secret labs, a creature that later escaped to be mistaken in Russia and Eurasia for a "snowman," or a relict hominoid?

People's Republic of China

The noted British novelist, screenwriter and director Stephen Gallagher revealed an interesting bit of information during an address given at the Wellcome Institute's symposium on the topic "Do Artists Demonize the New Genetics?" on March 23, 1995.

Gallagher had heard of a doctor in Shenyang, in northeast China, who claimed to have achieved success with the artificial insemination of human sperm to a female chimpanzee, only to have the three-month-old fetus destroyed by Red Guards who came in and smashed up his laboratory.

Scientists in China have created embryonic chimeras, hybrid embryos that contain human and rabbit DNA. On September 7, 2001, a report in

Beijing Youth Daily stated that Professor Chen Xigu in the Experimental Animal Center of Sun Yat-sen University had transferred a skin cell nucleus from a seven-year-old boy into a rabbit's denucleated egg and created an embryo. The aim of his research, according to the paper, was to use cloning to develop cures for such illnesses as diabetes and Parkinson's disease.

Apparently, with the growing numbers of scientists and medical centers engaged in similar experiments in China (such as the Shanghai Second Medical University), there is also a growing debate over the ethics of cross-species reprogramming.

Italy, 1987

A very interesting article, headlined "New breed of half-ape 'slave' thought possible," was published in the May 14, 1987, issue of the *Houston Chronicle*. Brunetto Chiarelli, dean of anthropology at Florence University, claimed that he had knowledge of a secret experiment in which a chimpanzee egg was exposed to human sperm with the result that an apparently viable embryo was created. The experiment was interrupted at the embryo stage because of ethical considerations. "Scientific information is numerous but reserved. Maybe at the end of the year we will have an idea of what has been achieved," Chiarelli said. Apparently, the cell proceeded to divide; it was the beginning of a routine developmental process that could potentially have resulted in a human-chimpanzee hybrid.

Italy, 1990s

Another fascinating document from the declassified Soviet archives confirms that noted endocrinologist Sergey Voronov conducted experiments on great apes in the 1920s. Voronov lived in a special facility in Grimaldi, Italy, a center he established known as "The Simian Castle." This animal preserve could contain 100 animals at a time. Voronov was searching for a formula to enable him to slow down the process of aging. He also conducted experiments to increase male virility and researched organ transplantation.

Voronov published a book about sexual cell transplantation from apes to humans.

Ventimiglia is a small Italian town on the Ligurian Sea and the Italian Riviera, near the French border. In nearby Grimaldi are grottoes in which prehistoric remains have been found. Strange creatures were sighted in this area in the 1990s, resembling the crossbreed of a primitive man and a gorilla. They were naked and stood two meters tall, with long hair, human-looking heads, large hypnotic eyes, and wrinkled skin.

Did Voronov create chimeric creatures whose descendants wander in the wilderness around the Italian Riviera? There is little available information about the enigmatic Russian surgeon. Did he know of Ivanov and his research? Italian sources state that the Russian scientist tried to "graft bodies of animals on human ones."

United States

According to an article in the October 27, 2003, issue of *U.S. News and World Report* ("Mixing species—and crossing a line?"), U.S. scientists have placed human neural stem cells into the brains of fetal monkeys to see how well these cells formed brain tissue. The cells thrived and migrated through the brain. The experiment drew little notice at the time. Nell Royce, the author of the article, wrote that today the experiment would spark more debate.

Scientists in Advanced Cell Technology, an American biotechnology company in Massachusetts, had previously (1998) mixed human cells and cow eggs in an attempt, similar to the Chinese experiments described above, to make hybrid embryos as a source of stem cells. The genes activated and the egg began to divide in the normal way up to the 32-cell stage at which it was destroyed. According to a number of American newspapers, those experiments were not successful.

Ethical Concerns

Nowadays the use of genetic engineering raises a number of concerns. By far, the greatest public concern is over the mixing of human and animal genes. After all, both cell fusion and recombinant DNA techniques allow species barriers to be readily overcome.

Human beings are changing the world at an ever-increasing pace. New crops appear almost every day. It is certain that we will be using genetic manipulation to change life forms themselves in the coming decades. Of course, we should be more alarmed about manipulation of animals than of vegetation and microorganisms.

There is a threshold of cross-species research that must never be stepped over, lest we walk into a minefield. We must not create situations where humans make life or death decisions without reference to God. We must be cautious not to create interspecies chimeras that would be able to replace or destroy *Homo sapiens.*

Chapter 20

The "Merlin" Who Guarded the Kremlin

Russian czars had court astrologers. One of them served Czar Basil II. An astrologer was present at birth of Peter the Great, and the Emperor later had an occultist among his entourage. The last Czar of Russia and his wife favored Grigoriy Rasputin. Stalin's Russia did not know astrology, and psychics were largely unknown, existing underground except for Wolf Messing (see page 133). In the 1930s, Stalin purged the KGB of those who researched the paranormal, and a number of the security service officials (such as Gleb Bokiy) were executed or sent to the Gulag.

The thaw came when Khrushchev assumed power. He had reportedly employed *ekstrasensi*-psychics as guards. Under Brezhnev, the Soviet population occasionally read about telepathy, astrology, ancient astronauts, and UFOS in the newspapers, and the *Samizdat* (underground) publications circulated, albeit in very limited numbers. Parapsychologists and healers such as Djuna Davitashvili treated the aging Soviet leaders. Andropov was very much interested in UFO research, and a controversial Russian astrologer

Count Sergey Vronsky claimed to have met some Soviet leaders while living in the USSR.

When the Afghan War was in full swing, psychics were in demand. The KGB had a scientific research institute, *Prognoz* (Prognosis), where scientists worked on projects to protect the state secrecy and research human psychic abilities.

After the Soviet Union disintegrated and Yeltsin assumed power, there were no more any barriers to the study of esoteric matters. The occult, astrology, and paranormal research were no longer taboo subjects.

Russia's Merlin

One of the most mysterious psychic personalities connected with Moscow's Kremlin is former KGB Gen. Georgy Rogozin. He was born in Vladivostok in 1942, and in 1969 graduated from the counterintelligence school of the Higher Intelligence School of the KGB. Later he completed post-graduate studies there. He served in the Pacific Navy as an intelligence officer. In 1978-80 Rogozin was a senior scientist of the operational analytic service of the Third Chief Directorate of the KGB, and later, he became deputy chief of the Prognoz Institute. Thereafter, his career in the KGB rapidly ascended. He was engaged in scientific and analytical work as well as research on the occult sciences. According to *Sobesednik* magazine (May 14, 2003) it was approximately in 1978 that Rogozin began working in the operational-analytical service of the KGB USSR Third Chief Directorate (military counterintelligence). The Third Chief Directorate performed tasks that extended far beyond counterintelligence to encompass extensive political surveillance of the armed forces and other military security duties.

Alexander Korzhakov, retired Lieutenant-General of the KGB, was once Boris Yeltsin's confidant and his closest adviser. For eleven years he loyally served the Communist reformist leader-turned-first-president of Russia. In 1992 Rogozin became his deputy and thus the second most important personality in President Yeltsin's security service. As the head of the Presidential Security Service, Korzhakov was often accused of interfering in governmental affairs. The powerful service gathered evidence on high government officials engaged in corruption and other crime.

It is possible to discern, from a number of interviews, that Major-General Rogozin was directly responsible for astrology and occult sciences in the President Yeltsin security service.

There have been numerous rumors in Russia about the man nicknamed "Merlin" by his colleagues. It was said that he could read people's thoughts and possessed telekinetic powers. He could move heavy tables using his mind; that is, causation by mental processes. The general, others said, claimed to have the power to travel back in time via "immersion" and predict the future. Rogozin discussed the influence of the Sun, Mercury, and other luminaries on political leaders. He also supplied Yeltsin with horoscopes and created a positive energy field around Russia's president. Rogozin sought out psychics and mind readers throughout Russia.

According to the former KGB officer and a consultant to FSB (modern Russia's security service) Yury Malinin, President Boris Yeltsin maintained a department of psychic security to protect himself from outside psychological influence and control. Some of Malinin's revelations were published at the Siberian news agency site.

The need to protect Yeltsin arose when a listening device was found in the government building; however, it was determined that this was no microphone, but a directed antenna, installed there to generate psychological influence on Russia's president.

General-Major Ratnikov, the first deputy director of the Main Directorate of defense of the Russian Federation in the early 1990s, saw the antenna and knew how it worked, but did not know who had operated the device. He and Korzhakov had tested similar devices in Afghanistan. In 1991 the antenna disappeared from Yeltsin's office.

Malinin claimed that Yeltsin's guards and security personnel closely protected him from magical foes, as well as devices that could influence his health. Over twenty Russian scientific institutions had researched and built such devices; the programs for their creation and coordination began in the late 1980s, and were headed by former intelligence high ranking officers.

Furthermore, Malinin claimed in another interview (*Komsomolskaya Pravda* newspaper, May 3, 2007) that he had searched all over Russia for the most capable psychics and was able to find ten powerful people who protected Yeltsin. They had projected energy into the president from a distance, maintained his weakening health, and warded off evil. But they had never come into contact with the president.

Rogozin mentioned that Malinin had collected information about scientific developments in the area of "psi-technologies" and rapidly growing ranks of psychics in Russia, but the general did not know how Malinin used his findings.

Ratnikov said that he and Rogozin analyzed threats to Yeltsin arising from magnetic storms and similar natural developments. While Rogozin saw Yeltsin's horoscopes, the president was never shown them; they were used for planning purposes. But there were no fortune tellers around Yeltsin, and many of those psychics who now claim they protected the president were never even introduced to him.

At the time, psychic devices were in vogue in Russia's murky political scene, and there existed specific price lists for such devices. Russian politicians paid money for ESP protection, as well as means to "charm" the populations of various towns to vote for them

Rogozin revealed much about himself in the interview given to Yelena Svetlova in 1999 (*Komsomolskaya Pravda*). He admitted that his team of experts had "immersed" into the past during their experiments as far as 135,000 years. They visited Central Asia and the cave people of the period. This was done using self-hypnosis. He also said that it was possible to look into the future, and that Russia in the year 2012 would be a more stable place. But Rogozin would not provide prognoses about the near future; he cited ethical reasons. However, the general claimed that his team knew in detail, via computer results, that on June 20, 1996, Korzhakov and the rest of the security service would be gone, purged by Yeltsin after Korzhakov challenged Russia's Prime Minister Chubais.

Rogozin revealed that the best secret agents are those born in the Year of the Monkey. He mentioned that he did not have to be close to Yeltsin because the general possessed psychological techniques to influence a person from distance. Such techniques, he revealed, were in the possession of Mayan Indians, the Aztecs, and some African tribes, as well as ancient Russians.

To preclude assassination attempts, emotional breakdowns among the Kremlin guards and others who provided security, as well as other factors that could affect the president, Rogozin's team paid close attention to those closest to Yeltsin. They used astrology, "soft" hypnosis, and gestalt therapy in their arsenal. This helped relieve the stress of the security personnel.

After Rogozin lost his position in the Kremlin, he became a consultant for strategic planning for several Russian banks, and later engaged in the PR consulting of the Economic Security Agency at the Trade Industrial Chamber of the Russian federation. Currently, the former Major-General of the KGB is a member of the anti-corruption subcommittee of the Russia's Public Chamber. He has a Ph.D. in Jurisprudence.

Legends and rumors surrounding Rogozin's four years tenure in the Kremlin have not as yet subsided. Meanwhile, the former KGB general also heads the Institute of Experimental Psychology, located in one of the buildings of Russia's Ministry of Energy. It is not clear whether he was the creator of the Institute, or as some sources indicate, it was Soviet leader Leonid Brezhnev who ordered that this be done (*http://www.astrologya.ru/index.php?id=26*).

According to Olga Vandisheva, a reporter with the *Komsomolskaya Pravda,* who interviewed him (June 13, 2003), Rogozin does not look like a wizard. He also denied that he practiced astrology, but did confirm his passion for the occult matters. Specifically, the general is interested in ancient Asian knowledge pertaining to control over human beings and the application of such knowledge in modern times. Considered as "dark science" in Russia, the results obtained from ancient knowledge were positive. As long as Rogozin's people were close to Yeltsin, the President suffered no failures. They also used "sleepers," those who can see the future in their sleep (a state of soft hypnosis). Currently, Rogozin and his people work with people who possess phenomenal powers: those who can read human thoughts from distance and those who can see through walls.

Rogozin claimed that Putin, whose sign is the Dragon, will rule Russia until 2012. This does not come from a horoscope; they use other technologies in the Institute. It is possible to see into the future, Rogozin believes. Nostradamus was able to see it, and apparently the former general claims to be able to as well.

Nazi Archives

V. Bogdanov published an article about the secret SS archives in *Rossiyskaya Gazeta* (August 5, 2003). A secret conference of astrologers and clairvoyants of the Third Reich took place in the Wartburg Castle to discuss Germany's future. The conference was held on the initiative of Joseph Goebbels; there were twelve active participants. An SS unit and a special group of Gestapo's radio and radio-technical technicians served as the guards at the conference. They possessed state-of-the-art means for interception, and Reichsminister Joseph Goebbels could hear everything that the professional magicians of Germany had to say at the conference. Unfortunately, no records of the conference and its participants exist. Recent discoveries made by those who research WW II and the Third Reich's history raise questions whether it was possible that some materials from the secret conference of magicians in 1938 became available to the Allies. American forces seized Thüringen in April 1945, and Soviet troops entered the area in the fall. It is possible that the Americans had enough time to question the local population and study the labyrinths of Wartburg Castle. It is known in Russia that the Soviet army took a unique device as a trophy. It was a coronograph made by order of

Hitler. The device was made not for investigation of solar activity, but for military and political astrological forecasts. The device was out of order. When Soviet engineers repaired it, the device was sent to an observatory near the Russian city of Kislovodsk, but Bogdanov did not know why. He also mentioned that unnamed sources ("people who would know") told him that Rogozin has used the captured SS archives of the occult sciences.

Here is another fascinating historical detail about Nazi archives: After Nazi Germany was crushed, Soviet intelligence services researched information they obtained from the files of the chief of the Nazi Abwehr military intelligence service, Admiral Wilhelm Canaris, a shrewd, brilliant spymaster. He was executed after joining with other high-ranking German officers in a dangerous plot to eliminate Hitler. Canaris was an enigmatic personality and a serious researcher of the occult in the Nazi regime. But there is no confirmation that Rogozin had access to Abwehr's files.

The Merlin's Foe

Rogozin's adamant opponent, Academician Eduard Pavlovich Kruglyakov, who resides in Siberia, is a Deputy Director of the Budker Institute of Nuclear Physics and heads the Russian Academy's Commission against Pseudoscience and the Falsifications of Scientific Studies. He does not mince words. He has tremendous knowledge of the subject (*Komsomolskaya Pravda,* May 3, 2007; *Izvestiya;* and other sources). He knew about the KGB Prognoz Institute. In his interviews, he describes Rogozin's team as "charlatans." The KGB general had tremendous powers and brought the "magicians" into the Kremlin. Enormous governmental expenditures were used for their programs: political horoscopes and so on. The academician does not know whether Rogozin actually believed them, but Yeltsin apparently did. He recalled the instance when in 1991 the Russian president visited Novosibirsk and was escorted to thermonuclear plants in an institute. Yeltsin asked the scientists if energy could be obtained from rocks. When Kruglyakov tried to explain that it was impossible, the president said that he was assured that it actually was possible. Kruglyakov then said that Yeltsin was advised by charlatans and the president was offended. Later the academician learned that Yeltsin authorized the expenditure of 120 million rubles to study the possibility of obtaining energy from rocks. But Kruglyakov is equally critical of programs in the United States (such as telepathy to maintain communications with submarines).

He claims that Rogozin began his research of the paranormal in the late 1980s (specifically, long distance mind-reading), and that the KGB general had an obsessive hobby: magic, occultism, and astrology.

Powerful Personality

Rogozin admitted that he had never worked with Yeltsin directly; he was way below him in the hierarchy. He provided information to those who were close to the president. His astrological interpretations were taken into account by his chief, Korzhakov, and by Yeltsin. The horoscopes were prepared for the president, as well as his guards, drivers, and others who surrounded him. Wild rumors helped the growth of Rogozin's standing in the Kremlin. In 1996 he became deputy head of the President's re-election campaign and was kept employed even after Korzhakov was fired. The day after the re-election campaign, Rogozin was thrown out, too. His colleague in the re-election campaign was Col. Pavel Sviridov, one of Russia's leading astrologers, fluent in several languages including Chinese, founder of School of Scientific Astrology, a PR expert and jurist, and consultant for various private and governmental agencies. He has been engaged in astrology for over twenty-seven years (under Communist rule, he claims that he was an "underground practitioner"). Sviridov considers Rogozin to be a very powerful personality who loves authority (*http://www.ctp.ru/*). But he also considers Rogozin and the group he represented to be amateurs in astrology. The horoscopes provided by them came from pirated discs, purchased on street corners. Sviridov claims that Yeltsin was aware of that.

Not long ago, Rogozin's speech from September 2006 was published as an article (*http://www.relga.ru/Environ/WebObjects/tguww.woa/wa/Main?textid=1312&level1=main&level2=articles*). The title was "Corruption as threat to the civilized development of civic society."

Perhaps he is now using his alleged powers to fight a very tangible threat to the future of his country.

The Kremlin Today

Putin does not care about astrologers, and they consider him to be a "dark horse." Yury Malinin stated that Putin is not defended against "psychic contamination" and his staff does not include professional "psi-guards." But that does not faze Putin whatsoever.

Part Five
Secrets of Russian Air and Space Exploration

The STAL-6 aircraft designed by Robert L. Bartini.

Chapter 21

Invisible Aircraft of Stalin's Russia

During the 1930s, a most unusual project was carried out in the Soviet Union. If it had been successfully completed, the map of the world would be quite different today.

In those times, a mysterious man named Robert L. Bartini lived in the Soviet Union. He was a genius who designed airplanes, but today we know little about his research. It is almost impossible to find detailed information about the man and his ideas in history books that deal with Soviet aircraft construction. Even specialized reference books do not mention him. But Bartini's research and development projects were sensational, even by our modern standards. Even before World War II, in the late 1930s, he was developing a supersonic bomber. He also created a physical theory about the multidimensional space-time continuum. The theory was a logical continuation and development of Einstein's Theory of Relativity.

Perhaps most fantastic, however, are the findings of Russian author S. B. Buzinovsky, who studied Bartini's life and published an article on him in 1993 in *Vsyo vozmozhno* magazine. Buzinovsky is of the opinion that Bartini directly participated in the development of an invisible Soviet aircraft.

Could this be possible? I was intrigued and decided to conduct some research of my own. Using Russian military sources and numerous reference books, here is what I found:

Robert Lyudvigovich Bartini (1897–1974) was a Soviet aircraft designer. A member of the Italian Communist Party since 1921, he moved to the Soviet Union in 1923. He joined the Communist Party of the Soviet Union in 1927.

Bartini created more than ten experimental airplanes, among them the DAR (long-distance Arctic reconnaissance airplane) and the STAL-6. Bartini also published books about aerodynamics and theoretical physics.

People who are familiar with the Russian aircraft industry were reluctant to discuss Bartini's work with me. My sources told me that if they asked questions about the invisible aircraft, they felt as if they had entered forbidden territory and touched upon a taboo subject.

Nevertheless, I was able to find some rather fascinating information. Twenty years ago, I. Vishnyak published an article entitled "Invisible Flight" in the Soviet magazine *Izobretatel i ratzionalizator*. Five years later the article was reprinted in the Soviet magazine *Tekhnika Molodezhi,* a prestigious scientific publication that also publishes investigative journalism.

Vishnyak's article contains the following description of an invisible plane:

"The unusual had occurred immediately after the engine started to operate. People waited for it: rumors that the thing to wait for was the start-up of the engine had spread through the base; therefore, the onlookers remembered all details. They heard the obligatory command, attenuated by the distance:

"'Away from the propeller!' and the reply, 'Yes, sir, away from the propeller!'

"Then the first blue streams of exhaust shot out from the ports on the sides of the cowling and at once, simultaneously with the increase of revolutions, the airplane began to disappear from view. It looked as if it waned, dissolved into air. One could determine that the aircraft was moving, taking off, and ascending only through the transference of the noise toward the forest and over it."

R. L. Bartini.

When did all of this happen? Vishnyak states that the event dates back to the second half of the 1930s. But where did the flight take place? "One of our northern airdromes" was as much as the Russian journalist was willing or able to reveal.

There is confirmation that the flight of the invisible aircraft actually took place. Prof. V. B. Shavrov mentions the flight in the first volume of his *History of Aircraft Design in the U.S.S.R.* Shavrov is a well-known historian of Soviet aviation. He states that the airplane was built by a brigade from the Military Air Academy under the leadership of S. G. Kozlov in 1935. The design was actually an adaptation from AIR-4, an airplane built by Yakovlev, a famous Soviet aircraft designer.

The aircraft's main feature was the sheathing of its surfaces with a transparent material. Rodoid, as it was called, was organic glass made in France. In addition, the Soviets used an original smoke screen—smoke or blue-colored fog that made the plane invisible against a blue sky. Shavrov also mentioned that the transparent surfaces of the airplane were covered with plate-glass amalgam from the inside.

Here is how Shavrov describes the test of the invisible airplane: "The airplane in flight quickly disappeared from the sight of the land-based observers. Test flights of the invisible airplane were conducted next to the UT-2 airplane, at a certain distance. Film sequences did not show the airplane, and at great distances, one could not even discern spots. However, with the passage of time, the plexiglass rapidly waned, and the invisibility was reduced. When the tests were completed, the airplane was disassembled and all work on the project was stopped. There was a design for a special invisible airplane with the framework of chromium-plated piping."

S. B. Buzinovsky has proposed the hypothesis that Bartini had made a discovery in the area of superpowered magnetic fields. He had discovered a previously unknown effect that can change the physical properties of a space-time continuum at one fixed point. This would allow an object (for example an airplane) located in the fixed point to become invisible to outside observers. Buzinovsky compares this to the famous Philadelphia Experiment. He has discovered that Bartini was interested in the physics of the space-time continuum and came up with his own corresponding theory.

Alexander Sergeyevich Yakovlev, a brilliant Soviet aircraft designer, was born in 1906. In 1946 he was promoted to the rank of lieutenant colonel. Yakovlev graduated from the N. E. Zhukovsky Military Air Academy in 1931. Then he worked as an aircraft engineer.

In 1935, Yakovlev became chief aircraft designer. Between 1940 and 1946 he also served as deputy People's Commissar of the aviation industry. Yakovlev became an academician at the Soviet Academy of Sciences in 1976. He directed aircraft design projects that resulted in the creation of various types of aircraft: the Yak-1, -3, -7, and other fighter planes, the BB-22, Yak-28, and training aircraft UT-2 bombers. He also created the first all-weather interceptor, the first Soviet-made vertical take-off and landing aircraft, and numerous passenger airplanes and various helicopters.

It is quite possible that Yakovlev worked hand in hand with Bartini.

What stopped the Russians from creating an invisible airplane that could be mass-produced? In 1935 Soviet dictator Joseph Stalin was poised to grab total control of the Soviet Union. The Great Terror was yet to begin, but the concentration camps had been operating in the U.S.S.R. since 1918. Hundreds of thousands of Russians of all faiths and backgrounds had been murdered by Communists. Stalin knew what was happening in the military design bureaus, and he most certainly was aware of the terrible potential of an invisible aircraft.

Did Yakovlev and Bartini stop the tests of the aircraft because they feared that Stalin would misuse their creation? Hardly. The two were dedicated Communists and certainly Soviet patriots. They would not have kept such powerful weapons away from Soviet arsenals when the Nazis invaded their country in 1941. Most likely the tests really stopped when they discovered that they couldn't sustain the aircraft's invisibility.

Modern technology and scientific achievements may well be able to remedy the invisibility defects. That could explain the secrecy surrounding Bartini's name, his theories, and his work. It is quite possible that the Russian military-industrial complex has gained control of Bartini's papers. If the story is true, the tale of the invisible aircraft is far from over.

Chapter 22

Russian Martian Secrets

A handful of Mars-bound spacecraft were lost in the last decade of the twentieth century. In the late 1980s two spacecraft from the former Soviet Union disappeared in the same "neighborhood." Both of the space probes contained laser devices.

Phobos, an international project, was devoted to the investigation of Mars and its satellites. The Americans were eagerly and effectively helping with the project. Two interplanetary probes were launched to examine the Martian moon Phobos. The Soviets were interested in using Phobos as a staging post for a manned exploration of Mars. Phobos 1 was lost on its way to the Martian vicinity; Phobos 2 reached the moon Phobos and carried out some experiments before it was lost—or annihilated.

Among the images the second Soviet probe sent back, before it malfunctioned—or was destroyed by a huge UFO—was one (and, allegedly the last one) that appeared to show a large object near Phobos. Analysis of this picture, and of a picture showing what seems to be the shadow of the "UFO" on Mars, reveals an object about twenty kilometers long.

Each probe contained a complicated set of devices: three television cameras, a spectrometer guidance system, and a video recording system. The onboard video spectrometric system (VSK) was created by international cooperation of scientific and industrial facilities from the USSR, Bulgaria, and the German Democratic Republic.

The international team, including Scientists from the USSR, Bulgaria, Germany, Finland, Great Britain, and the U.S, processed TV data. But Phobos 2 also contained a strange laser device, the Laser Mass Spectrometer Analyzer (Lima-D), built by experts at the Leningrad Institute of Precision Mechanics in collaboration with Finnish and East European scientists. The device was set to emit a laser ray at the surface of the moonlet Phobos in order to cause a mini-explosion and gather data on the evaporated substances.

Ten years go by, and another spacecraft is sent to Mars, the Polar Lander. On board it contains a strange device, the Light Detection and Ranging (LIDAJ) instrument provided by the Space Research Institute (IKI) of the Russian Academy of Science, under the sponsorship of the Russian Space Agency (RSA). This is the first Russian instrument to fly onboard a U.S. planetary spacecraft.

The LIDAR instrument was to look "for ice and dust clouds." The LIDAR system was a laser sounder located on the Mars Polar Lander deck and composed of sensor and electronics assembly. The LIDAR transmitter uses a gallium-aluminum-arsenic laser that emits energy in pulses at a constant rate and wavelength.

The LIDAR had two sounding modes—active and acoustic. During active sounding, the instrument sends out pulses of light and then times their return in order to locate and characterize ice and dust hazes to a level of two to three kilometers. An acoustic device, the Planetary Society's Mars Microphone was on the LIDAR assembly.

It is my belief that whoever dwells on Mars and its moonlets just does not like lasers, or any other devices onboard the spacecraft from Earth. With the exception of professional space scientists at NASA, JPL, and the Russian Space Agency, we know very little about the true nature of such lasers.

Chapter 23

Soviet Lunar Secrets

In the late 1960s I was a Soviet high school student in the city of Kiev. Igor was a buddy of mine, a teenager from a privileged family. We attended school together for a year or two. His grandfather, it was rumored, was a retired high-ranking military officer and a Communist Party functionary. Igor was not very open about his relatives, but I suspected his grandfather served in the state security and intelligence services, the KGB.

The old man's apartment was located in the new housing development of Borschagovka. It was full of expensive foreign-made furniture, vases, paintings, and books. Even the Soviet books I saw there were out of the reach of mere mortals like myself. But Igor let me borrow some of the books. He had an excellent collection of science fiction and adventure novels. Igor and his mother lived with his grandfather. I never knew what happened to Igor's father—the subject was taboo. When I left the Soviet Union, I tried to correspond with Igor, but he never wrote back. I recall that he wanted to have a military career in the rocket forces.

Once, Igor told me during a conversation about Americans landing on the Moon. "We beat them to it," he said. "We were first."

"Yes," he reiterated, "we reached the Moon before the Yankees did."

He did not go into detail, and I thought that it was a strange and foolish thing to say. Oh yes, we the Soviet people did reach the Moon, Mars, and other planets long before the Americans did—in our science-fiction novels—but in reality?

Not that I was against beating the Americans. I was a typical Soviet teenager, after all. But because I lived under the same conditions that most other Soviet citizens did, I was also aware that our Soviet motherland could not make properly working TV sets, frying pans, and steam irons, much less a rocket to land people on the Moon and bring them back to Earth. I was proud of the Soviet space exploration achievements, but I also heard hushed-up rumors about horrible failures and perished cosmonauts.

My colleague, Konstantin Kovalkovsky, is a noted UFO researcher as well as the publisher of *Spekrra*, a St. Petersburg newspaper. He runs a UFO phenomena research organization called UFONIKS. Not long ago I received information from him. After reading it, I recalled my conversation with Igor.

Kovalkovsky sent me an interview that was published in 1991 in *Megapolis Express*. The interviewer was Alexander Sidorko, a journalist. The interview subject was an ex-KGB officer named Vadim Petrov. He was responsible for the safety and the secret identities of Soviet cosmonaut-testers.

Test pilots exist in any nation that makes its own planes or has an air force. But few people, stated Petrov, knew about the Soviet cosmonaut-testers. Those who knew included the general secretary of the Communist party, the chief of committee for state security (KGB), Vadim Petrov, and a number of physicians, designers, and operators—never more than fifteen people. This was one of the most guarded secrets of the stagnation era (prior to Gorbachev's rise to power), and it apparently remains top secret.

The detachment of cosmonaut-testers was created even before Yuri Gagarin's flight. The idea came from the then-chief of the KGB, Semichastniy. It seems that the KGB was not certain that the automatic equipment on unmanned stations was reliable. The prestige of the Soviet Union depended on those space flights. Soviet unmanned space stations had to fly faultlessly and always complete their missions. Thus, it was decided to equip some of the stations with pilot modules, so that cosmonauts could control the flight through manual control and then report all collected data upon their return. The KGB chiefs reasoned that having human beings in control would provide them with two-hundres-percent safety for Soviet space flights.

The detachment accepted only volunteers from the KGB. The volunteers were invited for a discussion after the initial selection process that is best described by the Russian word *zaochno*, that is, without the volunteer's knowledge. All volunteers who were talked to, including those who did not make it into the detachment, signed statements of secrecy—the triple zero, the highest degree of secrecy in the USSR.

Vadim Petrov did not know anything about the testers' initial flights. His work with the detachment began in 1969. That was the time of the Lunokhod (Moonwalker) project. Lunokhod was a Soviet-made Moon exploration vehicle. The whole country was proud of this Soviet machine.

The two cosmonaut-testers who were being prepared for the flight to the Moon were number 13 and number 14. Therefore, Petrov guesses that prior to the Lunokhod project there must have been a dozen other flights. The testers in the detachment never revealed their true names.

All those associated with the Lunokhod project knew that numbers 13 and 14 would never return to Earth. They were to remain in a separate module. Upon landing on the Moon, their mission was to find Luriokhod, repair the chassis, align the tuning of solar batteries, and provide the corrected directions for television cameras. Number 13 and number 14 made those famous lateral shots of the Lunokhod vehicle.

When the testers were being sent to the Moon, some seasoned KGB officers associated with the project cried. But the two volunteers were no cowards, according to Petrov. They guided the station to its target and accomplished all the Lunokhod program projects. This was very likely the most tragic episode in the history of Soviet space exploration.

If Petrov is to be believed, then how did my friend Igor come to know of the detachment? Was his father somehow connected to the detachment? Did Igor's grandfather play a role in it? Apparently Igor knew something, for he was always calm and collected, and he did not like fantasy or tall tales. Were the volunteers really so determined to sacrifice their lives for the glory of the Motherland? I doubt it.

The KGB knew the true situation in the Soviet Union better than anyone else, and they were quite cynical. They preferred to keep on living their lives rather than die for Brezhnev's projects. I believe that their psyches had been changed, that they became victims of Soviet mind control experiments: they became space zombies, able to carry out assigned tasks but not to ruminate on why the tasks had to be carried out. It is interesting to note that at about this time, the Soviets made a popular motion picture titled *Experiment Doktora Absta,* about Nazi projects to turn POWs from various navies into human torpedoes, mindless beings that guided German torpedoes against Allied ships.

Dr. Kang Mao-kang, a scientist in communist China, is a leading astrophysicist. According to Kovalkovsky, the Chinese scientist had received information from a "reliable source in the USA," along with photographs of a human footprint and a human skeleton on the surface of the Moon. In the winter of 1988 Mao-kang showed the photographs to a conference of journalists in Beijing. *The New York Times* carried the story in its October 17, 1989, edition. Mao-kang claimed that he had once possessed documents and letters to prove the footprint on the lunar surface was quite recent, and that the skeleton was unquestionably human. Only the Americans can provide the information, said the Chinese astrophysicist (the photographs allegedly were taken by the crew of Apollo 11).

If what Mao-kang said is true, was the skeleton number 13 or number 14? Could it be that the answer to the riddle actually lies in some Russian filing cabinet? I believe that there are no real experts on Soviet and Russian space exploration in the U.S. We have no choice but to wait for the secret files to be declassified.

Chapter 24

UFOs and the Aborted Mission of Soyuz 18-1

Oleg Makarov, a cosmonaut, scientist, writer, and twice decorated Hero of the Soviet Union, died in Moscow in 2003 from a heart attack. His colleague who had flown two space missions with him, scientist and cosmonaut Vasily Lazarev, died of alcohol poisoning in 1990.

The secrets of the aborted Soyuz 18-1 mission still remain unsolved. I have been following the story for years, and I have collected some fascinating facts about the unusual 1975 mission to the Salyut 4 station.

The mission is referred to in the literature as Soyuz 18-1 (sometimes Soyuz 18a) since the following Soyuz mission in May 1975 received the name Soyuz 18. In the Soviet Union, only successful missions were given numbers...

That year the Soviets wanted to compete with the U.S. Skylab missions and establish their own space-station program. Cosmonauts Vasily Lazarev

Oleg Makarov and Vasily Lazarev.

and Oleg Makarov were selected for the Soyuz-1 mission. Both were distinguished personalities. Makarov, a graduate of the Bauman Moscow Higher Technical School, had worked in Special Design Bureau Number One under the legendary Sergey Korolyov. He was selected to be a cosmonaut in 1966. Makarov was engaged in the Soviet lunar program (later cancelled), and was training for the circumlunar flight. He participated in the Soyuz 12 spaceflight in 1973. Lazarev was the mission commander. This was the first Soviet manned mission in the wake of the Soyuz 11 tragedy during which three cosmonauts were killed during reentry. Makarov and Lazarev returned to Earth safely after two days in space.

In later years, Makarov worked for RSC Energia (former Special Design Bureau) on the MIR space station and the Buran shuttle development.

Lazarev, a colonel of the Soviet Air Force, a fighter pilot, a surgeon, and a Ph.D. in medicine remained a cosmonaut until the 1980s, but he did not fly again after the abortive Soyuz 18-1 launch he commanded. They were tough, those two cosmonauts. And they knew how to keep secrets, too.

UFO Sighting at the Baikonur Launch

The Vostok-1 spacecraft with the world's first space traveler was launched from the Baikonur Cosmodrome, the world's oldest and largest operational space launch facility, fourteen years earlier. So much had happened since then. The year 1975 was an important one for space exploration.

On the morning of April 5, preparations were underway for the launch of the Soyuz-18-1 spacecraft. The weather was clear, and the cosmonauts that comprised its crew felt great. Their mission was to reach the Salyut-4 orbital station, relieve the crew of Sergey Gubayov and Georgi Grechko, and work at the station for sixty days.

According to the retired Soviet Col. Gherman Kolchin, a respected author and researcher who has excellent connections, a few minutes before the Soyuz 18-1 launch, Lt. Col. V. Ilyin had observed a cross-like object of a transparent-grayish color hovering at a great altitude in the sky, over the launching area. While he and his chauffeur watched the peculiar object, the rocket was launched. The officer recalled that the weather over Kazakhstan is usually clear some 270 days a year and he could clearly observe all phases of the rocket flights. At the 120th second, the *bokovushki* (boosters) separated in a proper fashion and flew off to the sides in a cross-like manner. Lieutenant Colonel Ilyin recalled that, after that, one could observe a luminescent dot without using any optical enhancement, indicating that an engine was working, and then the dot disappeared. At the 150th second, the nose flailing (*golovnoy obtekatel*) separated. But this time, after the *bokovushki* separated, the rocket made a very strange trajectory that was clearly discerned by the inversion trail.

So only minutes into the flight, separation problems occurred with the Soyuz booster.

Ilyin remembered the "grayish cross" he had observed in the zenith. But the object was not there anymore. His chauffeur, Gena, confirmed that he, too, saw the grayish cross.

Vladimir Ajaja, Russia's eminent ufologist, mentioned this episode in his book *Inaya Zhizn* (Moscow, 1998). He added that we would probably never find out whether the ill-fated UFO had any role in the failure of the mission.

But there are other questions about this doomed mission that we may never find out.

The Doomed Flight

The four strap-on boosters separated, followed by the nose flailing and the escape rocket. At 261 seconds after liftoff, the time came for the third stage to break away from the second stage. It was then that the cosmonauts encountered a violent swaying motion followed by a loud siren and a red *avariya nositelya*, "booster failure," warning light on the control panel. The third stage had only partially separated, although it had ignited right on schedule, thus threatening to send the spacecraft crashing onto the taiga below. The crew sent repeated requests to mission control to initiate the abort sequence. Finally, Soyuz-18-1 was separated from the wayward booster. Hence the spacecraft's main engine engaged and pulled clear. The spacecraft's descent module separated from the rest of Soyuz at altitude. Following a ballistic trajectory, Lazarev and Makarov were subjected to a horrifying 20g re-entry, twice the normal g-load. The cosmonauts most likely suffered injuries as a result. But then the deceleration forces decreased and their spacecraft's parachute system was activated, as well as soft-landing rockets. And so the Soyuz command module containing the exhausted crew was separated from the booster, and having plunged back to Earth came to rest on an Altai mountainside.

According to Ajaja (and the official report), the suborbital flight had lasted 21 minutes and 27 seconds, reached the altitude of 192 kilometers, and flew 1574 kilometers altogether.

Vadim Ilyin's Article

Russian journalist Vadim Ilyin (probably no relation to the Lieutenant Colonel Ilyin mentioned above) published an article in issue 16 of *NLO*, a popular St. Petersburg magazine, in 2004. "*Kosmonavtov spas NLO*" (Cosmonauts were rescued by a UFO) was the article heading. Ilyin claimed to reveal heretofore unavailable information.

He stated that at 260 seconds, the voice of P. Klimuk, the communications operator at mission control, was cut off, and the crew heard nohing but noise interference for a moment. Then they heard Klimuk's voice again, but it was weak It sounded as if someone (or something) unsuccessfully tried to imitate to imitate human speech. The cosmonauts thought that such noises could be produced by a computer that would try to relay some information through the use of vocal chords. They could not understand the contents of the transmission. A few seconds later they heard the siren and saw the warning light on the control panel.

According to Vadim Ilyin, the cosmonauts heard the same strange sounds again after 270 seconds of flight. Communications with the control center were sometimes normal and at other times were subdued. Then they heard the sounds of an awkward imitation of a human voice. They could not understand the meaning of the transmission, and wondered how an outsider could connect to the radio communication channel designated exclusively for the crew's and the mission control center's use.

The Landing Site

There have been questions as to where exactly the two cosmonauts landed. It was near the town of Gorno-Altaisk (1,600 kilometers from Baikonur), not far from the border with Red China. According to some sources, the cosmonauts believed that they actually landed in China, at that time their country's adversary. When they opened the hatch, the cosmonauts found out that they were surrounded by a snow-covered landscape, that their capsule was held by a parachute (caught in a tree according to some sources, and caught by a rock ledge according to others) over a ravine five to six hundred meters deep. Makarov managed to fix their whereabouts and calculated that they had landed in the Altai Mountains (some two thousand kilometers from Baikonur). And yet, to be sure their secrets did not become Red China's prize, according to some sources, he and Lazarev burned flight documents. The cosmonauts, although suffering from the consequences of their landing, nevertheless managed to crawl outside. Vadim Ilyin stated that they were so exhausted that they could not move. Some time later the cosmonauts recovered somewhat. They put on their thermal clothing, and after burning the documents, switched on the distress signal. They crawled in the deep snow, gathered some twigs, and were able to light a fire. The temperatures that night were sub-zero.

UFO Sighting

Vadim Ilyin states that not long after the cosmonauts lit the fire, the night fell. Airplanes (not just one) flew over them, signaling that the landing site was found, and flew away.

The wind chased away clouds that arrived in the evening and then grew calm. Suddenly Makarov and Lazarev heard an increasingly loud whistling sound, and at the same time they saw among the stars some luminescent object hovering right above them. They could neither determine its shape nor its altitude. They observed a bright spot, glittering with violet color. The object hovered over them for about half a minute, and then, as if confirming that all was in order, it disappeared as suddenly as it had appeared. According to Vadim Ilyin, Lazarev told German journalists in 1996, while in London on a private visit, that he has since been certain that not only did they observe a UFO that night, but also that a UFO had tried to contact them using their communications channel. He added that he thinks it was only because of the object's interference that they had landed in the Altai Mountains in one piece and without harm, in the area that resembles the Moon more than the Earth. Asked by journalists as to why neither he nor Makarov said anything about the UFO upon their return to Baikonur, Lazarev replied that in those times, should the cosmonauts reveal that they had observed unknown objects in the sky or some supernatural phenomena, they would have been excluded from any future flights. He added that the tape containg recordings of all their communications with the mission control center had been carefully studied. He never knew about the results of the study, but he did learn that the tape had disappeared under unclear circumstances.

There is one very clear circumstance that negates Vadim Ilyin's story: Vasili Lazarev died in Moscow, December 31, 1990, of alcohol poisoning, six years before his supposed London visit.

Oleg Makarov died in Moscow, May 2003, of a heart attack.

Was it a typo in Vadim Ilyin's article in *NLO* magazine, and the year of Lazarev's visit to London was actually 1986? If so, who were the German journalists who interviewed him? Whom did he visit in London?

The Geologist

L. Smirenniy, a scientist at the Research Center of Radiation-Chemical Safety and Hygiene, Moscow, and academician at the International Academy of Astronautics, was once a cosmonaut himself. Excerpts from his memoirs were published on the *Nauka I Zhizn* website (issue 5, 2007). He recalls speaking with a distinguished and legendary Soviet test pilot, Hero of the Soviet Union, S. N. Anokhin. He worked in the S.P. Korolyov design bureau and headed a team of "test-cosmonauts." Anokhin revealed to Smirenniy that having analyzed all of Makarov's actions that fateful day, he found that the cosmonaut behaved with exceptional courage.

Smirenniy, who had trained at the centrifuge (at ten-g), realized that after the twenty-g reentry the cosmonauts would suffer consequences to their health. Makarov told him that the mission commander Lazarev was not able to find out from the mission control center about the landing site. It seemed that the center did not hear their inquiries. Lazarev asked his engineer to determine where they would land.

"It would be China or the Pacific Ocean," came back Makarov's sarcastic reply, who added some strong Russian expressions about the failed mission. They did not know that their conversations were transmitted; the center heard them, but they could not hear the mission control center. Makarov's opinion about the engines' emergency performance enraged V. P. Glushko, who was the general designer of the mission and chief developer of the engines. He ordered the transmission of communications to be limited and stated that Makarov would never fly again. He was wrong.

Smirenniy added that the cosmonauts were initially discovered by geologists. They flew to the slope in their small helicopter, and a young man jumped out. He trudged through deep snow, reached the cosmonauts, and offered his help. The rescue helicopter arrived in the evening hours, and because of the darkness, could not take the cosmonauts away. The three of them spent the night in freezing temperature. The next morning their rescuers had returned, but the helicopter commander said he could not take a stranger. Makarov firmly stated that they would not leave without the geologist, and the rescue helicopter took all of them aboard.

Lazarev would have mentioned the geologist in his recollections if he had ever actually spoken to German journalists about the UFO they allegedly sighted that night.

Conclusion

We probably will never find out what really had happened in April of 1975 during the failed Soyuz 18-1 mission. That mission was the only case of a manned booster accident at high altitude.

Vasili Lazarev never flew again aboard Soviet spacecraft. He was discharged from the cosmonaut corps due to illness and remained a colonel in the reserves.

Oleg Makarov had two more flights into space, the last in 1980. The aborted Soyuz mission was dubbed the April 5 anomaly, and the Soviet government did not acknowledge it until April 7, 1975. Both cosmonauts were eventually awarded the Order of Lenin for their conduct, despite efforts by officials who sought to deny them that honor, and because of the personal intervention of Leonid Brezhnev they were given monetary compensation for the use of the emergency escape system.

Chapter 25

Sinister Dirigibles over Russia

Strange, cigar-shaped objects have been seen in the sky over Russian cities, villages, testing grounds, battlefields, forests, and secret installations. Surely many observations have been lost in the whirlwind of history; however, I have been able to collect some striking reports:

1915

Unknown dirigibles were seen at the mouth of the Volga River, over villages and towns covering a distance of 150 kilometers. A huge, dirigible-like balloon with a roaring motor and spotlights shining down was observed in the sky over the Kazan Military District. A finned, cigar-shaped object hovered over a village. Six humanoid shapes were seen in a "boat" under the object's "belly."

On September 26, the Kalmyk prince Iseren Badmayev saw what appeared to be a puff of black smoke appear from behind a hill and split into two parts. Each part, initially spherical, assumed an elongated shape in the

A 1907 French military dirigible.

blink of an eye. Both resembled gray boats. One part moved southward; the other headed west. For several minutes, the prince watched them move high above the horizon in the cloudless sky. He saw another "boat" about forty minutes later. He reported that the vehicle in which he was traveling at the time stood still each time he saw a boat in the sky.

A search-and-capture expedition was dispatched, but the objects were not found. The unknown aircraft appeared to be harmless, and General Sandetsky, Commander of the Kazan Military District, paid little attention to the reports, though he did inform the Supreme Command General Headquarters and the Russian General Staff. When he received no response, the documents were shelved in the archives for future reference.

Similar reports came from towns more than eight hundred kilometers north of Astrakhan and even from the Ural Mountains. An October 9 report from the village of Baranovka mentioned a landing in the forest.

Information about the sightings, based on extracts from the files of the

Central State Military Historical Archives of the USSR, was reported in the April 1991 edition of the now-defunct magazine *Soviet Soldier.*

1940s

Retired Col. Gherman Kolchin, a respected researcher, published an article in *NLO* magazine in 2000. It mentioned recollections of A. Kovalchuk, a lieutenant colonel during World War II. A huge, dirigible-like object 100 to 150 meters long passed over the military airfield where Kovalchuk was stationed at an altitude of five hundred meters. Air defense units fired on it with cannons and machine guns to protect the airfield. The object, which had no gondola, disappeared into the distance unharmed.

1953

Veniamin Dodin, a writer, military scientist, and lecturer, was in exile in Krasnoyarsk Kray, Siberia, not far from the site of the famous Tunguska explosion of 1908. On a clear night in June, while walking, Dodin heard a high-pitched noise that seemed to be coming from inside his head. He clearly saw a long, gleaming, cylindrical craft hovering over clouds about two miles away. Its rotating, drum-shaped body was girded with something that resembled a moving staircase with many steps. Dodin immediately assumed it was a dirigible, but was confused by the absence of cabins or cockpit. As the slowly rotating object approached him, its design appeared to be technologically incorrect. He assumed it had come from the testing area of the nearby top-secret Soviet research center known as "Box 26," where new types of super-powerful weapons were being developed. The flat, drum-shaped end of the object that faced him separated itself from the cylinder and ascended rapidly, making a painful squeaking noise. Several more flat drums followed suit. Then the open end closed and the mysterious cylinder flew away. The flat drums disappeared and Dodin's earache went away.

The "dirigible" returned the following night. Dodin knew that no conventional man-made object could travel at such velocities as to instantly disappear from view. Was the object some advanced aircraft? He worried that those who ran the sinister Box 26 would come to the area. Inmates of local concentration camps and other exiles like him had heard horrible rumors about the projects of the secret research center. Knowing that if he were caught taking photographs in the forbidden Oimolon area he would be sent back to the Gulag camps or worse, Dodin nevertheless photographed the object and watched the sky for more than forty hours as other, similar objects appeared.

The smaller, flat drums poured out of the 650-foot motherships. Each drum appeared to be about eighty feet in diameter and polished. Each mothership threw out eight perfectly smooth, flat drums. Dodin used a Zeiss theodolite to observe the strange objects. He had no other tools. The eyepiece he looked through enabled him to discern a slight luminescence emanating from the panels of the drums. The mothership did not emit any luminescence. Dodin tried to reach the site of the nearest cylinder. He failed every time. Moreover, he became ill whenever he approached the site. Prior to the incident, Dodin was never ill in the taiga. Now he experienced sharp pains in his joints. He once again heard the same sharp, painful noises as on the first night and was forced to turn back. As soon as he came home, Dodin fell asleep for a long time.

The MVD (the KGB of the period) arrived in the area in early July, accompanied by Soviet military pilots. They confiscated Dodin's camera and film and questioned him extensively. These actions convinced Dodin that he had photographed some top-secret Soviet project, but he found out later that he was wrong. The objects had troubled Soviet military commanders in the area, too. They had tried to use radars, but had discovered that something was jamming their radar station. The super-high-frequency radiation emanating from the mothership was so great that the MVD and pilots decided to evacuate. Before fleeing the site, however, they ordered Dodin to continue his observations.

According to Mark I. Shevelyov, who headed the Arctic Aviation Agency,

Soviet leaders quickly learned about these UFOs but decided to refrain from challenging the unknown. Stalin had died not long before, and the situation in the USSR was not very stable. However, the Soviets blinked, and on August 7, 1953, their airplanes attacked the UFOs over Ishimba. Their air-to-air missiles were inexplicably turned away from their UFO targets and fell to earth, burning a gigantic area of the taiga. Two interceptor aircraft and their pilots and copilots vanished. All radar equipment within a 120-mile radius of the site broke down. Dodin's radio made a piercing noise and shut down. Then a horrible noise hit Dodin and he fainted. He regained consciousness at night. When he climbed outside his hut, he discovered a world painted in greenish hues. The luminescence in the area remained greenish for more than a month. It faded slowly, like radiation after a nuclear explosion. Dodin would never forget that evening.

1954

At 8:12 a.m. on August 17, an unusual object was sighted by an anti-aircraft unit guarding a missile battalion very close to the Chinese border. Their radars registered strange interference. A few moments later, an object resembling a rocket was observed, but it had no stabilizers and moved horizontally at low speed. Its movement resembled that of a dirigible. Three missiles were fired at it. They exploded before reaching the target. The object rapidly ascended and soon disappeared.

A commission from the Ministry of Defense arrived the next day to investigate. Because its members found no objective reasons for missiles having been fired under the circumstances, the commanding officer of the missile battalion was removed from his position.

1956

V. Fomenko (who would later become one of Russia's leading ufologists) and other witnesses observed a gigantic, cigar-shaped UFO over a secret testing range in Krasnoarmeysk, near Moscow. The object hovered for two and a half hours. Fomenko measured its altitude at one hundred kilometers, its length at about one kilometer, and its diameter at approximately one hundred meters.

1965

A Soviet nuclear submarine was to rendezvous with a ship in the Atlantic Ocean. It arrived at the meeting place an hour and a half before the appointed time. The captain allowed the crew to come outside on deck. No ships were in the area and the sky was starry and cloudless. Then the watchman observed a cigar-shaped object moving noiselessly through the sky.

Although the submarine was in international waters, the crew assumed the object was American-made, so they prepared to dive immediately. But when onboard radar did not register anything, the captain decided to stay on the surface. When three rays suddenly shot out from the UFO, the witnesses noticed that it had no gondola and no horizontal or vertical rudders. The object was about 200 to 250 meters long. Soviet submariners were not familiar with such "dirigibles." Those used by the American Air Force were much smaller.

Then something strange took place: the UFO slowly descended to the surface of the ocean, its searchlights still on, and dived under the water about half a mile from the submarine. The submarine's sonar registered a strange, intense hissing sound of very short duration as the UFO submerged. All the witnesses were ordered to report the details and provide drawings to the Special Department (i.e., naval intelligence).

1970

One night after secret launches of new rockets at the Kapustin Yar test range, the shouts of alarmed sentries awoke others. A gigantic, dirigible-like object was hovering in the clear, starry sky over the remaining rockets. It emitted a thin, green, needle-like ray, as if sensing the rocket positions. When a sentry panicked and fired at the UFO, the ray vanished and several soldiers screamed in pain with horrible headaches.

1970s

Col.-Gen. Gennady Reshetnikov, Chief of the top Command Academy of the Air Defense Forces, is a former Commander of the Air Defense Forces of the Soviet Far East. Valery Uvarov, a Russian ufologist, interviewed him for the Russian newspaper *Anomaliya* (Issue 3, January 30, 1996). Reshetnikov mentioned several interesting incidents when aircraft were scrambled after UFOs. He investigated the sighting of a cigar-shaped craft with portholes that occurred in the late 1970s over the Arctic area of Norilsk. It visited the area several times, alarming the military.

Reports issued by Adm. V. A. Domislovsky, chief of the Pacific Fleet's Intelligence Department, described a gigantic cylindrical object sighted by the Soviet Navy in "faraway" regions of the Pacific Ocean. The object was eight hundred to nine hundred meters long. When it hovered over the ocean, smaller objects exited from one of its ends like bees from a beehive and descended into the water. Some time later they reentered the gigantic UFO, which flew away and disappeared over the horizon.

1981

Mark Shteynberg, a Russian-American journalist and a former Soviet officer, reported that a gigantic UFO appeared over the air-defense regiment of the Soviet 12th Army in August. The area is close to the Iranian border, in the town of Kizil-Arvat. The Russians were vigilant and nervous because Iraqi forces were fighting the Iranians; this was also during the Soviet-Afghan war.

The strange elliptical object hovered at an altitude of seven kilometers. Two MIG-27 jets were dispatched to pursue it. The UFO slowly and noiselessly moved northward. The radar registered it without any problem. The captain who flew the leading interceptor told ground control that he had the UFO in sight. Ground control ordered him to fire two missiles at the target. The UFO disappeared at great speed. The leading interceptor and the missiles it had fired also vanished instantly. No traces of the plane or its missiles were ever found on the ground.

The cigar-shaped UFO was approximately one hundred to two hundred meters long. A special commission investigated the incident and confirmed all the facts in the report prepared by the regiment's commander. As a result, the commander was demoted because he had issued orders to intercept without asking his superiors (*Vestnik,* Issue 3, 1992). His argument that he had been justified because the sighting took place so close to the Iranian border (a mere one hundred kilometers) was not accepted.

S. N. Komlev, a Soviet scientist, was a trained meteorologist with professional experience in the observation of atmospheric meteorological phenomena and flights of weather balloons. In 1985 he sent a UFO report to a recently established commission for the study of anomalous phenomena. The incident had taken place at the end of September 1981, at about 12:15 a.m. Moscow time. Komlev, a passenger aboard a TU-134 flight from Balkhash to Moscow, observed a cigar-shaped object. The airplane at that time was flying at eight hundred kilometers per hour in the vicinity of the Vnukovo Airport, at an altitude of approximately eight thousasnd meters. The white-yellowish object was seen through the portholes by almost all of the passengers. No one could identify it. Komlev estimated that it was about the size of an airplane hull viewed from a distance of two or three kilometers. Apparently the object paced the TU-134 about thirty kilometers above it. The observers could not determine the direction of the flight. They saw no residue or inversion. No sections or components were noted and no effect on humans or onboard equipment was detected. The atmosphere at the time was transparent; one could see the stars and the ground. The sighting lasted about two minutes, then the airplane changed course and the object was not seen again. The plane was not allowed to land for an extended period of time. Komlev believed this was a consequence of the UFO sighting.

1982

M. L. Gaponov was a noted Soviet scientist involved in geophysical and biomedical research and a participant in international geophysical scientific expeditions to the North Pole. He personally observed a gigantic, cigar-shaped UFO hovering over the Gagarin Cosmonaut Training Center at Zvezdny Gorodok (Star City), the USSR's only school for cosmonauts.

1987

Dalnegorsk, a small settlement in the Far East of Russia, is the site of the famous UFO crash of January 1986. On Saturday night, November 28, 1987, at 11:24 p.m., thirty-two flying objects appeared from nowhere. Hundreds of military and civilian witnesses saw them. The objects flew over twelve different settlements, and thirteen of them flew to Dalnegorsk and the crash site. Three of these hovered over the settlement, and five illuminated the nearby mountain. The objects moved noiselessly at an altitude of 150 to 800 meters.

As the objects flew over houses, they created television interference. Ministry of Internal Affairs officers testified later that they observed the objects from a street. One was a cylindrical object the width of a five-story building and two hundred to three hundred meters long. It flew straight at the quarry, its front part lit up like burning metal. Quarry workers were afraid it would crash on them. A quarry manager named Levakov observed it slowly moving at an altitude of three hundred meters. He stated that he was well acquainted with aerodynamics, but never knew that a body could fly noiselessly without any wings or engines.

1989

Phobos 1, the Soviet space probe sent to Mars in 1988, was lost that September on its way to the red planet. Phobos 2 arrived in orbit around Mars in January 1989. On March 28, 1989, TASS, the official Soviet news agency, announced that Phobos 2 had failed to communicate with Earth as scheduled after completing an operation around the Martian moon Phobos, and was lost. Marina Popovich, a famous Russian test pilot, author, and researcher, while visiting Los Angeles in 1991, showed this author a photograph that Phobos 2 had taken just before its demise. It depicts a cylindrical object approximately twenty-five kilometers long. After that last frame was radio-transmitted back to Earth, the probe disappeared.

In 1919, man crossed the Atlantic in a dirigible, a journey of 5,800 kilometers, but even today no man-made dirigible is capable of separating itself into two autonomous craft. And we certainly do not have dirigibles twenty-five kilometers long that are capable of space flights to Mars!

Where do the mysterious cylinders come from? Where do they fly away to?

To order additional copies of this book,
please send full amount plus $6.00 for
postage and handling for the first book and
$1.00 for each additional book.
Minnesota residents add 7.125 percent sales tax

Send orders to:

Galde Press, Inc.
PO Box 460
Lakeville, Minnesota 55044-0460

Credit card orders call 1–800–777–3454
Fax (952) 891–6091
Visit our website at *www.galdepress.com*
and download our free catalog,
or write for our catalog.

Printed in Dunstable, United Kingdom

80913565R00127